Practicing Military Anthropology

Practicing Military Anthropology

Beyond Expectations and Traditional Boundaries

Edited by Robert A. Rubinstein, Kerry Fosher, and Clementine Fujimura

Kumarian Press
An Imprint of Stylus Publishing

Practicing Military Anthropology: Beyond Expectations and Traditional Boundaries

COPYRIGHT © 2013 by Kumarian Press, an imprint of STYLUS PUBLISHING, LLC.

Published by Stylus Publishing, LLC
22883 Quicksilver Drive
Sterling, Virginia 20166-2102

All rights reserved. No part of this book may be reprinted or reproduced in any form or by any electronic, mechanical or other means, now known or hereafter invented, including photocopying, recording and information storage and retrieval, without permission in writing from the publisher.

Front Cover Image: August 7, 2007—A donkey loaded with medical supplies and humanitarian aid leads the way as members of the Panjshir Provincial Reconstruction Team begin a 2,000-foot descent into a river valley. PRT members made an 11-mile round trip trek to provide medical care to Afghans living in Roydara village in the Shutol district of Panjshir province, Afghanistan.

Library of Congress Cataloging-in-Publication Data
Practicing military anthropology : beyond expectations and traditional boundaries / edited by Robert A. Rubinstein, Kerry Fosher, and Clementine Fujimura.
    p. cm.
  Includes bibliographical references and index.
  ISBN 978-1-56549-548-7 (cloth : alk. paper) — ISBN 978-1-56549-549-4 (pbk. : alk. paper) — ISBN 978-1-56549-550-0 (library networkable e-edition) — ISBN 978-1-56549-551-7 (consumer e-edition)
  1. War and society. 2. Anthropological ethics. 3. Applied anthropology. 4. Military ethics. I. Rubinstein, Robert A., 1951– II. Fosher, Kerry B. III. Fujimura, Clementine K., 1965–
  GN497.P73 2012
  306.2'7—dc23
                                                                           2012012905

13-digit ISBN: 978-1-56549-548-7 (cloth)
13-digit ISBN: 978-1-56549-549-4 (paper)
13-digit ISBN: 978-1-56549-550-0 (library networkable e-edition)
13-digit ISBN: 978-1-56549-551-7 (consumer e-edition)

Printed in the United States of America

All first editions printed on acid free paper that meets the American National Standards Institute Z39-48 Standard.

Bulk Purchases: Quantity discounts are available for use in workshops and for staff development. Call 1-800-232-0223

First Edition, 2013
10 9 8 7 6 5 4 3 2 1

Contents

Acknowledgments		vii
Preface		ix
Introduction: Exploring Military Anthropology		1
Robert A. Rubinstein, Kerry Fosher, and Clementine Fujimura		
1	Archaeological Ethics and Working for the Military	9
	Laurie W. Rush	
2	"Living the Dream": One Military Anthropologist's Initiation	29
	Clementine Fujimura	
3	A Day in the Life of the Marine Corps Professor of Operational Culture	45
	Paula Holmes-Eber	
4	The Road Turnley Took	65
	Jessica Glicken Turnley	
5	Pebbles in the Headwaters: Working Within Military Intelligence	83
	Kerry Fosher	
6	Ethnicity and Shifting Identity: The Importance of Cultural Specialists in US Military Operations	101
	Christopher Varhola	
7	Master Narratives, Retrospective Attribution, and Ritual Pollution in Anthropology's Engagements With the Military	119
	Robert A. Rubinstein	
References		135
Editors and Contributors		141
Index		145

Acknowledgments

We are grateful to Christopher DeCorse, chair of the Department of Anthropology at the Maxwell School of Citizenship and Public Affairs, Syracuse University, for suggesting we undertake the symposium, "Anthropology and the Military: Charting the Future of Research and Practice," in May 2008 that resulted in most of the chapters in this volume, and for finding the funding that allowed us to hold it.

Brian Selmeski and Kerry Fosher devoted themselves to the design and management of the symposium. They both worked on assembling and editing the initial drafts of the chapters. Kerry Fosher, who works for the US Marine Corps, and Brian Selmeski, who works for the US Air Force, took time from their demanding jobs to work on the symposium. While we prepared the chapters for publication, Brian was instrumental in establishing the Air Force Culture and Language Center based at Air University in Montgomery, Alabama. Because of the duties associated with that work, Brian found he could not devote as much attention as he would have liked to bring the symposium papers to publication. Indeed, his professional commitments have kept him from contributing his own chapter to this volume.

Although Brian had to turn his attention elsewhere, we want to acknowledge the extremely important role he played in making the symposium happen, and in his contribution to the initial editing of this book. We appreciate too that when his other commitments became so demanding that he could no longer give his full attention to this volume he relinquished his editing role, allowing the project to move forward. Without his efforts we would not have been able to reach this point.

We want to thank all of the contributors for their chapters, for their work in revising them, and for their forbearance with the process of moving this book to publication.

We would like to thank the faculty and students of the Department of Anthropology at Syracuse University for attending the symposium presentations and especially for their contributions to the ensuing conversations.

Finally, we would like to thank and acknowledge the partial financial support for the symposium by the Dean's office of the Maxwell School.

Preface

The relationship between anthropologists and the US military has commanded much attention during the past six years. Conversations at professional meetings, in the pages of disciplinary journals, and in books have been heated. Sometimes these conversations have been nasty and polemical. Perhaps this was especially so at the 2007 annual meeting of the American Anthropological Association (AAA), where in a session titled "The Empire Speaks Back: US Military and Intelligence Organizations' Perspectives on Engagement with Anthropology," organized by Kerry Fosher and Brian Selmeski, participants spoke about their work studying military culture and about their efforts to introduce cultural understanding into the curricula of various professional military education settings.

The following day at the AAA's annual business meeting, a person rose from the floor to speak passionately about anthropology's engagement with the military. He said, "Yesterday there was a panel called 'The Empire Speaks Back.' Everyone on that panel is a war criminal and should be banned from the association." There was applause at this remark. Charging anyone with being a war criminal and proposing sanctions as a result is a serious act. Yet, no objections to this comment were made by anyone on the floor or by those presiding over the meeting. We discuss this event further in chapter 7.

The next day Robert Rubinstein, who had participated in the panel, and Christopher DeCorse, chair of the Department of Anthropology at the Maxwell School of Citizenship and Public Affairs, Syracuse University, discussed the panel and the reaction to it at the business meeting. We noted that much of what was being written and said about military anthropology and military anthropologists seemed to be based on supposition rather than empirical investigation. Chris suggested that our department hold a two-day seminar for practicing military anthropologists to come together to discuss what they do and how they came to do it. As we refined the idea of a symposium, it seemed to us that its design would be best undertaken in cooperation with Brian Selmeski and Kerry Fosher, both of whom had recently completed their doctoral degrees in our department and were working with the military. Working with Robert, Brian and Kerry took the lead in designing the framing documents for the symposium and in making up the roster of invited guests.

Kerry was serving as a member of the American Anthropological Association's Commission on the Engagement of Anthropology with the US Security and Intelligence Communities, and the three of us had received invitations to participate in conferences about the militarization of anthropology. So we knew that a number of efforts were underway to confront the ethics of working with the military and to consider what a disciplinary perspective on working with the military in the current moment ought to be. Several of these meetings were energized by and focused on the Human Terrain System (HTS), an Army program that deploys teams including social scientists to provide cultural information to commanders in Iraq and Afghanistan, because the ethics and disciplinary dangers of the HTS seemed to be dominating much of the conversation and thinking about military anthropology.

Yet, we knew that whatever the involvement of anthropologists with the HTS, it did not characterize the work and activities of the majority of military anthropologists. So we determined that the Syracuse symposium could make a unique contribution by providing a venue where military anthropologists could discuss what they do and how they came to do it.

To this end, we invited participants to reflect upon their current professional situations and to narrate their stories about going to work with the military. We wanted the symposium presentations to be personal and informal. We provided participants with a guiding framework but asked that they be creative in tracing their evolution as military anthropologists. All the participants were asked to write in the first person. Several have chosen to experiment with a literary approach to convey a sense of what life is like for them as they work for the military.

This book is intended to begin to provide answers to the question, Who are military anthropologists and what do they do? The chapters should be of interest to a wide variety of people. We think they will be especially useful for advanced undergraduate and graduate students who are considering what shape their future careers might take and wish to have a better sense of the challenges and rewards that come with working as a military anthropologist. We think the chapters in this volume will also be interesting and helpful for professional anthropologists who want to better understand this area of applied work and to have a sense of the multiple professional pathways military anthropologists can take.

In conversations about military anthropology, it is not uncommon to hear that PhD anthropologists working in military settings are no longer actually anthropologists. Rather, they are said to be *technicians* of the state. We hope that one of the results of reading the chapters in this volume will begin to soften the sharp edge of this distinction. In addition to giving insight into the personal journeys of the contributors, their chapters detail the ways their anthropological training shaped them as professional anthropologists and continues to inform the way they think about their work lives.

It is worthwhile noting here what this book does not do. Over the past few years a number of volumes have appeared that seek to analyze anthropology's relation to the national security state (McNamara and Rubinstein 2011), to examine how anthropology articulates with "global counter insurgency" (Kelly et al. 2009; González 2009a), and to treat the ethics of military anthropology (Lucas 2009; Albro et al. 2011). While the contributors to this volume touch on each of these concerns, their main focus is unique. They provide deeply personal accounts of how one becomes a military anthropologist, what it means professionally and personally to pursue that path, and they discuss the day-to-day challenges they meet and how they respond to them. As such, the chapters in this volume provide a unique perspective on military anthropology and are a rich resource for better understanding the relationship of military anthropology to the wider discipline.

Introduction
Exploring Military Anthropology

Robert A. Rubinstein, Kerry Fosher, and Clementine Fujimura

In the United States the relationships among the military, individual anthropologists, and anthropology as a discipline are long-standing and complex.[1] At times these relationships have been characterized by cooperation, at other times by resistance. In between, there have been periods when questions about anthropological practice in relation to the military have been less resonant for individuals and the discipline. Especially as the nation has gone to war anthropologists have been more explicit and self-conscious in their relations with the military. The discipline has moved between engaging with what we now call *the security state* and advocating that anthropologists have nothing to do with that state.

For example, at its 1941 annual meeting during World War II, the American Anthropological Association (AAA) resolved that it "places itself and its resource and the specialized skills and knowledge of its members at the disposal of the country for the successful prosecution of the war" (Eggan 1942, 289).

Anthropologists became involved in the war effort in a variety of well-known and not-so-public roles (Price 2008). Some of these activities led to new understandings about how to conduct research and advanced our theoretical understanding of humans.

But at the same time the resolve to support the military was not unanimous. The objections to this collaboration congealed around three points:

- the tension between anthropologists' professional roles and their role as citizens,

- the harm that might befall the people among whom anthropologists studied as a result of anthropological cooperation with the military, and
- the tension between the benefits and harms that might come to the discipline as a result of that collaboration.

For example, writing in the *American Anthropologist* in 1942, B. W. Aginsky (1942, 521) warned, "For centuries man has endeavored to answer the questions concerning mankind. Gradually there has been established a body of scientific information which has broken down some of the prejudices and mythologies concerning man, and which has made it possible for man to attain an understanding and possibility of a better way of life. Today, all of the findings are being thrown into discard."

Writing in a similar vein, Embree (1945, 636) commented about the ways anthropology had been bent to the service of war work:

> A peculiar recent development midway between government work and the universities is a preoccupation with "national character structures," especially those of enemy nations. Some of the statements concerning Japan, for instance, made by this group are suspiciously reminiscent of the racism of an earlier day. There is a strong implication that because of our enemy's undesirable character structure and our own desirable virtues in this regard (plus better firearms), we have the moral right to walk in and reform, by force if necessary, the family life, education, and religion of peoples different from ourselves. A curious doctrine for the heirs of Franz Boas.

Aginsky's and Embree's articles expressed concerns that our social science knowledge should be put to "good" use, that the people we study should not be put at risk, and that the social sciences themselves would be damaged by cooperation with the military.

This latter concern is reflected in a series of papers from the AAA's Committee on International Cooperation in Anthropology published in the *American Anthropologist* under the general title "Anthropology during the War." These assess how anthropology fared during World War II, and whether in specific regions of the world the discipline was healthy or damaged (see, e.g., Herskovits 1945).

When Aginsky and Embree wrote, it could fairly be said that a survey of the discipline would have shown it was a period characterized by anthropological cooperation with the military.

Many anthropologists were deeply shaken by the dropping of the atomic bombs. For example, Margaret Mead was so affected by these events she set aside a book on which she was working. Her unpublished book developed an anthropological vision of a world in which progress and peace were constructed. As well, Robert Redfield and Sol Tax, among others, called upon anthropologists to recognize the dire threat to our species posed by the atomic bomb, to do what they could to halt nuclear proliferation, and if possible to "put the genie back in the bottle."

Through the 1950s a stable, if fragile, standoff developed between the United States and the Soviet Union. During this time anthropologists became especially concerned with the negative effects of colonialism and of Cold War imperialism on the peoples they studied, often those at the peripheries of power. American anthropologists became alarmed about the spreading militarism in our own society and the perils of American imperialism elsewhere. Anthropological writings during the 1950s and 1960s foreshadow more contemporary concerns. For instance, Jules Henry (1951, 135) wrote, "I would only add here that we cannot expect the friendship of the world if that friendship must come always in terms of our own symbols—which, by the way, we often betray at home."

Much of the conduct of international relations during the Cold War was shaped by disciplines other than anthropology. In this context, and in the belief that anthropology had something special to contribute to international security discussions, Sol Tax, with the support of the Wenner-Gren Foundation, invited anthropologists around the world to contribute their thoughts on the topic "Anthropology and World Affairs," with specific reference to the elimination or reduction of conflicts, by submitting papers and attending regional conferences.

To frame the discussion in a way that might produce responses that engage the policy community, the foundation circulated a packet of papers among anthropologists discussing conflict and nuclear deterrence from various policy-analyses perspectives, and Tax asked that each anthropologist "write a statement of his position with respect to arguments current in strategy and thinking on the grounds of his anthropological background" (Bunzel et al. 1964, 430).

The responses to this request also foreshadowed later debates, as some extracts from the unpublished summary of responses prepared by Robert

Wolfe from the University of Chicago philosophy department show (Wolfe 1963, 1):

> Several persons refused to discuss the question in terms set by the readings; others argued in considerable detail that the entire deterrence debate was a cover for economic, political, or ideological struggles. As anthropologists, as citizens, and as intellectuals, this group insisted that it could not fruitfully think about world peace in terms of alternative military strategies. . . . The language and frame of reference of the "dissenters" was indistinguishable from that of the more orthodox respondents. The keynotes were a rejection of ethnocentricity (or exclusive concern with a purely American point of view); a holistic approach to the cultures of the major powers; an insistence that war and international conflict were to be viewed as culture traits, or as institutions of a society, not as the consequences of this or that policy; that the long run, rather than the short run, is the appropriate perspective for viewing social phenomena; that the underdeveloped countries not directly involved in the cold war dispute contain truly significant problems for the future; and finally that if Anthropology can contribute anything to the current strategy debate, it is to broaden the scope and terms of the discussion, and divert attention from the minutiae of weapons systems to basic cultural and institutional determinants of the cold war.

By the mid- to late 1960s, in the context of the Vietnam War, relationships between American anthropology and the US military had largely reversed. A few anthropologists like Gerald Hickey (2002) worked in close cooperation with the military, but the majority of anthropologists joined Joseph Jorgensen and Eric Wolf (1970) in resisting involvement with the US military, finding it dangerous for the people anthropologists studied and for anthropology as a discipline. At this time the tone and tenor of debates about the relationship of anthropology to the military became quite fractious, dividing the discipline in ways that can still be seen today.

The relationships among the US military, anthropology, and anthropologists has risen to prominence again in the wake of the United States' invasion of Iraq in 2003. At first that invasion seemed a smashing military success, as planners predicted. Soon after, the situation changed. An Iraqi insurgency became quite active, and the US-led coalition began to suffer significant setbacks. By 2005 officials of several branches of the US military concluded that the setbacks were caused by a significant lack of cultural understanding. They began to seek cultural expertise from anthropologists (and others) first about Iraq and later about Afghanistan.

The increased interest in anthropology from institutions of the national security state was a deep concern for many anthropologists. The AAA formed a Commission on the Engagement of Anthropology with US Security and Intelligence Communities (CEAUSSIC), on which Kerry Fosher served. CEAUSSIC issued its final report in November 2007 (Peacock et al. 2007), which made the distinction between anthropology *of* the military and anthropology *for* the military. However, the commission recognized that this distinction is problematic in that many people considered military anthropologists engage in both. Whatever the status of this distinction, the fact is there is a lack of ethnographic detail about what military anthropologists actually do when they work for the military.

This shortcoming has turned out to be a particular problem for a serious discussion about these relationships. As the report was being prepared, the Human Terrain System (HTS), which sought in part to embed anthropologists with military units so they could provide on-the-ground cultural advice, became a focus of attention for the discipline.[2] Especially after HTS burst into the discipline's consciousness in early 2007, many discussions were framed as though the work of HTS personnel was the norm. This made it extremely difficult to have well-informed debates about what anthropologists should and should not be doing. Soon, it seemed, any anthropologist who worked with the military, and many who studied aspects of military communities, was treated as though he provided combat support. This conflation meant that a few sensationalized cases and individuals became the common narrative thread in disciplinary conversations displacing deep and thoughtful treatment the topic requires (see Rubinstein this volume).

This volume seeks to address the paucity of written accounts of individual practice and decision making by anthropologists working in the security sector. It is difficult for those in the discipline to have a robust and thorough discussion about the appropriateness of a realm of practice if that realm is opaque to the majority of anthropologists.

By bringing together leading military anthropologists to reflect on their career paths, current activities, and challenges, this volume seeks to begin to redress this gap in the empirical understanding of military anthropology. Simply put, it seeks to start to form an answer to the question, Who are the military anthropologists, and what do they do?

The breadth of work undertaken by those engaged in studying and working for the military might be understood by analogy to specialized areas of anthropology, especially medical anthropology (Rubinstein 2011). Medical anthropologists use a wide range of approaches and work in many different areas, which coexist in some tension with one another. The range of theoretical approaches and venues of work vary and include clinically applied anthropology, applied medical anthropology, and critical medical anthropology. Importantly, it is not uncommon to find medical anthropologists working across perspectives—critical in one area but working clinically in another, as appropriate. In the same way, the distinction between anthropology of the military and anthropology for the military, which the CEAUSSIC found troubling, is, as Lucas (2009) notes, a distinction that fails to adequately capture the complex reality of the work done by military anthropologists.

Some of that complexity is reflected in the chapters in this volume. The contributors are from a cross-section of some of the several domains in which military anthropologists work: (a) education, for example, at service academies, professional schools, colleges and universities; (b) training, for example, in predeployment settings and professional development; (c) policy development, such as providing research or advice for policymakers and program developers; (d) intelligence, for instance, in the analysis of information and in the development of the parameters for the information to be collected; and (e) operational support, including deployment to the theater to provide insights for policy and programming and doctrine development, to conduct assessments of training, or to work in a reach-back cell (a resource outside of the area of operation that can be contacted for additional information). Thus, the stories they tell provide a broader understanding of the work of military anthropologists.

We asked the participants in the symposium "Anthropology and the Military: Charting the Future of Research and Practice" held at the Maxwell School of Syracuse University on 29–31 May 2008 to reflect in their presentations on a set of common questions using an informal and personal tone. All contributors were asked to present an ethnographic reflection on their development as individuals and as professional anthropologists, addressing the following: What personal experiences led them to work as military anthropologists? What kinds of training did they receive? What professional options did they consider? We also asked the contributors to reflect in that framework on the projects they have undertaken, to note any special challenges they might face in their work, and to comment on how they responded to those challenges.

The chapters in this book reflect some, but by no means all, of the complexity and variation in the community of anthropologists who have chosen to work with the military. This variation is not simply a matter of different organizations or job decisions. The contributors have reached their choice to engage and their styles of engagement from divergent points. They have been working with the security sector for different lengths of time and have chosen to write about their experiences differently. Some emphasize the way personal and intellectual histories have informed their engagement. Others highlight more recent choices and ethical decision making, along with the details of current work. As with all anthropologists across all topics, the degree of significance ascribed to current disciplinary debates varies. For some authors, the ongoing controversy about the ethics of working with the military is a key feature in how they think about their practice. For others, although they are aware of the issues being discussed, the debates play a far smaller role in their day-to-day professional lives.

As the reader will see, there are many commonalities and also many divergences in the contributors' stories. We comment on these in the brief editors' introduction at the beginning of each chapter. But here it is worth noting that many of the contributors describe personal histories of being fascinated by other cultures, which often carried over into an interest in the cultures of the military organizations with which they work. As all the contributors are anthropologists, this is perhaps the least surprising aspect of their stories, since nearly all anthropologists of any persuasion can report such an early fascination with the lives of other people. As we noted earlier, the discourse about military anthropologists often mark them as some kind of *other*. Yet, in the chapters that follow, the reader will see trajectories of professional education that are resoundingly similar to that of anthropologists working in other fields. Some of the contributors describe their doctoral educations with the mentorship of distinguished senior anthropologists, and they reflect on how this training affected their career choices and their thinking about the roles they play in the institutions where they work.

Anthropologists studying or working in groups of any kind interact with people. They build rapport with members of the groups with whom they work. Although they may report on societies or organizations as a whole, through their interactions with people, anthropologists come to recognize the diversity inherent in any group. Common to the chapters in this book is the acknowledgment that the contributors see their interactions with the military not only in terms of organizations or structures but also in terms of the individual people with whom they engage.

One theme woven through the chapters in this volume is that a core aspect of decision making among military anthropologists is that they work in deeply human contexts. Rather than considering ethical choices purely at the level of seemingly monolithic institutions—as do many discipline-wide discussions of the ethics of anthropologists becoming involved in the national security state—military anthropologists' deliberations involve the people who make up those institutions and that take place in diverse institutional settings.

This book is intended to provide a sort of ethnographic accounting of the lives and work of military anthropologists. Our goal is simply that it enlightens, enriches, and informs our disciplinary discussions of what military anthropologists do by providing case studies of the experiences of some colleagues in anthropology.

Notes

1. The views expressed in this work are the authors' alone and do not represent the position of the US Marine Corps or any government organization.

2. The HTS was an army program launched in 2007 to address the perceived need for social science research to support military commanders. Early forms of the program were designed around the concept of human terrain teams of social scientists and other personnel who would conduct field research and perform analyses to improve military commanders' understanding of the culture in Iraq and Afghanistan. Briefs on HTS focused on the inclusion of anthropologists and anthropological methods in these teams, although the program employed relatively few cultural anthropologists. A description of the HTS and its components can be found in the 2009 CEAUSSIC report (Albro et al. 2009).

1

Archaeological Ethics and Working for the Military

Laurie W. Rush

Laurie W. Rush describes the personal and professional pathways that led her to a career as a military archaeologist. She began with the military well before the wars in Iraq and Afghanistan generated interest in anthropology. She describes a series of ethical choices independent of the United States' invasion of Iraq. Rather, she discusses other issues of practice, such as treatment of skeletal remains. This chapter provides a valuable alternative perspective on the kinds of work anthropologists can do in a military context and is especially notable in that it addresses ethical choices and behavior in the current context beyond the preoccupations of an anthropologist working for the military. As she reflects on her own choices, Rush also writes of the ethical struggles of military colleagues and the implications for the discipline of how anthropological colleagues interact with one another when ethical issues arise.

All our decisions, large and small, compound like interest to form the essence of our lives. What was the sequence of choices that brought me to a tiny Army personnel office located in a somewhat shabby, renovated World War II "temporary" building? What preparation did I have to take an oath to defend and support the Constitution, so that I could begin my new job as an Army archaeologist? In early 2001 the United States was not at war. In fact, at that time the US military appeared to be evolving into a scholarship program, and the emphasis in military training land management seemed to be trending toward conservation and stewardship. It may be difficult to believe, but in 1998 large signs welcoming everyone to the installation read "Fort Drum, Dedicated to Preserving the Environment." The job I was poised to take offered the opportunity to manage a half million dollars a year to support archaeological predictive modeling, inventory survey, and site evaluation in one of the most interesting areas of the Great Lakes region. I was also being offered the opportunity to establish a Native American consultation program, and the Army had made it clear that my job responsibilities included advocacy for stewardship of and indigenous access to the hundreds of Native American ancestral places found on the 107,000 acres of Fort Drum lands.

Even with the clearly positive aspects of the Army archaeology program, the initial decision to work at a military base did not come easily. I came of age during Vietnam. College campuses had only just settled down from the riots of the late sixties when I started my career at Indiana University-Bloomington. At that time, my view of military personnel was inextricably intertwined with My Lai and Kent State. It seemed unimaginable to me that anyone with honor would willingly join the US military, and I felt infinite relief when my future husband's randomly drawn draft number was high enough to ensure that he would not be called to serve. In graduate school at Northwestern University, our academic community of anthropologists, faculty and students alike, appeared to be almost entirely composed of left-leaning liberals. As students, we were encouraged to request as much money as we possibly could from the federal government in the form of grants and loans while being admonished never to even consider working for this same government's Department of Defense (DOD). The National Science Foundation paid for my PhD, but no one in the anthropology department ever suggested that completing graduate school debt free was a privilege.

It is fair to ask what a person whose original career goal, as articulated in high school, was to use archaeological methods to study the legends of King Arthur and the Knights of the Round Table was doing in an anthropology graduate program at all. The Glenn Black Laboratory of Archaeology at Indiana University is an anthropology-based program dedicated to studying Native American prehistory. At the time, it did not occur to me to study classics or art history as a means to pursue my archaeological interests. Once engaged in anthropology as a field of study, I found all the subfields fascinating. As an undergraduate and MA candidate, I specialized in human osteology, a subfield of physical anthropology. My PhD dissertation was in medical anthropology. I returned to archaeology as a curator after an internship at the Field Museum in Chicago and as part of an adult lifetime of participant observation in a tiny rural maritime community on the St. Lawrence River.

My first experience working for the Army was through a contract with the Army Corps of Engineers to set up the artifact curation facility at Fort Drum in the early 1990s. The purpose of the contract was to ensure that Fort Drum was in compliance with the Native American Graves Protection and Repatriation Act of 1990. Archaeological inventory of the proposed cantonment construction for reactivation of the Tenth Mountain Division at Fort Drum had resulted in extensive archaeological collections that needed appropriate housing and a cataloging system. After two years of work and successfully establishing a curation facility, I observed that there were personnel problems among the Fort Drum environmental staff, whose root cause did not become clear to me until years later, encouraged me to return to college teaching and museum consulting.

In the spring of 1998, a friend who had become the Fort Drum archaeologist in the interim asked if I would consider returning as a consultant to write a long-range plan for the cultural resources program. As I worked on the plan, it became increasingly clear that morale in the program was low, and before long, both permanent archaeologists resigned and left. Representatives of the Environmental Division staff asked if I would step in as a contractor to run the program. When I seemed reluctant to accept, they pointed out that if I refused, the archaeology field crew would all immediately lose their jobs for want of a principal investigator. I accepted, and after a few months I realized that I liked the job, and I signed a long-term contract with the Colorado State University Center for the Environmental Management of Military Lands to run the Fort Drum program on a more permanent basis. My employer was a university, which created a comfortable employment situation for me, even if my job responsibility was focused on military land.

The reassurance of a university affiliation, however, was not destined to last. In the late 1990s, DOD staff were in the process of writing and establishing one of the most progressive and proactive Native American consultation policies to be found in all the federal agencies. In fact, as I write this chapter, DOD is celebrating the tenth anniversary of this policy. For me personally, what this policy meant was that as Fort Drum and the Tenth Mountain Division began to establish government-to-government relationships with federally recognized tribes with ties to Fort Drum lands, the archaeologist would need to be a federal employee who could represent the government. And so, in June of 2001, I found myself in an Army personnel office contemplating taking an oath I did not even know existed: *"I, [name], do solemnly swear (or affirm) that I will support and defend the Constitution of the United States against all enemies, foreign and domestic; that I will bear true faith and allegiance to the same; that I take this obligation freely, without any mental reservation or purpose of evasion; and that I will well and faithfully discharge the duties of the office on which I am about to enter. So help me God."*

This oath applies to all federal employees, not just military ones. Clearly, federal employees make an ethical decision as the first requirement of accepting a position with the US government. Considering the practical circumstances, I am sure I am not the only new federal employee who found herself in a personnel office on her first day of work being asked to take an oath she had not seriously considered. I certainly had not read the Constitution carefully in preparation. I do remember thinking about the fact that my husband's income provided a safety net that gave me the option of resignation if I needed it. In retrospect, since my thought process at the time included strategies for a way out, clearly I was not entirely honest when I affirmed that I was taking the oath without any mental reservation. At that point, the types of ethical challenges I was imagining were focused on the possibility that I might be pressured into providing archaeological opinions that would compromise preservation and stewardship.

The Army Archaeology Experience

Seven years later, there is no question that my experience with the US military has been quite different from my expectations. The stewardship question turned out to be a nonissue. The military leaders I have worked for have been extremely interested in the archaeology of the installation and committed to good stewardship of the military land entrusted to them. One of my favorite memories is of a two-star general whispering, "That is so cool!" when during my introduction as a luncheon speaker I was described as the installation archaeologist who had discovered sites on Fort Drum that were over ten thousand years old. In over ten years, for every critical decision concerning an archaeological or cultural resources issue, the military commanders I work for have without exception selected the site management option I presented as the optimal choice. We have protected hundreds of acres of archaeological properties and have established practices that assure Native Americans access to their ancestral places across the installation.

On an average day at Fort Drum, I attend project design meetings. I plan for future archaeological surveys. I answer management questions about Fort Drum's only standing historic district, the LeRay estate. I respond to inquiries from the public that range from genealogy requests to ghost stories, and I work with Range Control to make sure that training soldier needs are being met. I enjoyed college teaching, but given the option I would choose Fort Drum a second time. The opportunities for research and new discovery are difficult to match, and we have state-of-the-art imagery, remote sensing, and mapping tools at our fingertips. At any point, if I miss teaching I can pester the field crew.

It is hard to know what I might have accomplished if I had continued to teach anthropology at the college level or worked in a museum. However, the Army and Fort Drum offered the opportunity for me to lead an archaeology team that has discovered over two hundred precontact archaeological sites. Our geographic information system and imagery assets enable us not only to do effective predictive modeling but also to track and manage all our discoveries. Fort Drum models and management methods have been published in New York State Museum publications so our colleagues in the region can benefit from our work. The Army also encourages and supports our efforts to publish and present papers and posters at scientific meetings all across the United States.

In addition, a positive working relationship with garrison command has enabled us to set aside dozens of the most important archaeological sites for permanent preservation. A series of these sites yielded tool kits that are consistent with the possibility of maritime technology dating from the earliest occupation of our region, and the DOD funded research for comparing our results with archaeological discoveries at other military bases across the continent.[1] The paleomaritime potential at Fort Drum has even attracted the interest of eminent archaeologists like Dennis Stanford, who identified a possible relationship between the assemblages and landforms at Fort Drum and other potential paleomaritime sites in New England.[2]

Native American Consultation

As rewarding as the archaeological research has been, the most significant contributions have been made in my role as the Fort Drum coordinator for Native American affairs. As a young graduate student in the 1970s, I found the required field experience included excavation of Native American burial mounds in the lower Illinois River valley. Several weeks into the season, one of the teams discovered an individual buried alone at the edge of a mound. His survivors had placed a pipe in his hand. The idea of disturbing him troubled me but not nearly as much as it concerned my father. It happened that on this occasion, my parents were making the one and only visit they ever made to see me working on an archaeological site. When my father realized that I was involved with a project that was disturbing human burials, it was the only time in my life that I remember knowing he was ashamed of my behavior.

As soon as the required fieldwork ended, I made the decision that my career in anthropology would no longer include research on human skeletal material. This decision alienated my academic adviser and very nearly cost me successful completion of my PhD. From this experience I learned that when individuals participate in an activity they later determine to be unethical, even when done out of ignorance, the deed cannot be undone. I also learned to pay more attention to my instincts, especially when individuals in positions of power may have been rationalizing unethical behavior.

My master's thesis topic was in human osteology. I understand that much has been learned from studying Native American human remains. I also suspect that many archaeologists in the twentieth century may not have had a clear understanding of the Native American spiritual beliefs that cause such anguish to descendants when the ancestors are disturbed. Those of us who are raised in a Judeo-Christian tradition find it difficult to conceptualize a belief system in which the essence of the individual does not leave the physical remains after death. If there are cultures where physical remains are simply that, physical remains with no associated spiritual beliefs whatsoever, I might not see any ethical challenge to the excavation and scientific study of the bones of their ancestors. I also understand that I have many colleagues who disagree adamantly with my decision that the excavation and study of Native American human remains is unethical. I respect their opinions and still count some of them among my friends.

If we think about ethics in terms of the greater good, my personal experiences have led me to the conclusion that the knowledge gained by the scientific excavation and study of Native American human remains does not outweigh the pain that the practice causes living Native Americans. I have witnessed this anguish personally. My personal experience with human remains also raises a critical issue for teaching ethics in archaeology. During the course of my training, introduction to field school consisted of being taken to a site, assigned an area of responsibility, and being told to dig. There was no discussion of whether any aspect of the activity might be right or wrong or painful for others. From my perspective now, a key piece of my professional training was missing and a teaching opportunity lost. Students need to be offered multiple perspectives and given the opportunity and guidance to make informed ethical decisions about research protocols and potential careers. This guidance should come from faculty and professionals they respect, and it is critical that students be offered more than one point of view to consider.

Over the course of time, and especially after direct consultation with Native Americans, my personal feelings on the issue of Native American human remains have only grown stronger. The DOD offered the first opportunity in my career to work with Native Americans in an honorable way. The DOD Native American consultation policy emphasizes respect. When Native American heads of state make official visits to US military installations, they are offered the same protocol as any other sovereign government leader. The Native American affairs coordinator is expected to handle diplomatic relations and to provide the cultural expertise required to help the military leadership make Native American guests feel comfortable and welcome. When this job is done well, the heads-of-state meetings are usually productive and result in agreements and protocols governing the protection of ancestral places and human burials.

For some military commanders, cross-cultural communication comes naturally. One of our commanders of the Tenth Mountain Division, who hosted a heads-of-state visit, offered clan mothers and faith keepers a helicopter tour of ancestral places. Amid the demands of preparing for deployment, this major general took the entire afternoon and gave the delegates his full attention. He proved to be a most engaging and gracious luncheon host. This same commander endeavors to attend, in person, every funeral for a Tenth Mountain soldier who is lost in battle, and he never misses an opportunity to encourage members of the civilian workforce. One of my first thoughts upon meeting this individual was, I could follow this person into a war zone.

At Fort Drum, one outcome of consultation has been ceremonial access to an important cultural place where Iroquoians can gather for the first time in nine hundred years and teach their children about the wisdom of the ancestors. When I read literature that questions the ethics of an archaeologist who chooses to work for the military, I have noted there is no mention of the critical role military archaeologists play as advocates for the access of indigenous people to ancestral places located on military land, and no suggestion for who would fill that void if archaeologists resigned from the military as a form of political protest.

Ethics and Military Archaeology

If we lived in a world where September 11 was an ordinary day, ethics and military archaeology might not be receiving so much attention. Had I stayed "in my lane" and restricted my concerns about preservation to Fort Drum lands, it is possible that my personal ethical decision to work for the US Army might never have been questioned by anyone. For me professionally, the effects of September 11 struck in October 2004, when news of US military damage at Babylon hit the global media. At that point, the irony of protecting archaeology on domestic military land while deploying soldiers to world heritage sites in Mesopotamia became clear.[3] In addition, the journalists relayed the frustration with and criticism of the US military by academic archaeologists who work in Mesopotamia. Military archaeologists have extensive experience in teaching and implementing archaeological stewardship in the military setting. If military colleagues offered their knowledge of how to work effectively within the DOD to their angry colleagues in academia, there was potential for positive action and site preservation. Sometimes the option of taking no action can be unethical. In October 2004 it was clear that US military personnel needed more information about the archaeology of Mesopotamia. Given my experience and expertise as a military archaeologist, the option of not taking action never entered my mind.

I know that one of the ethical charges laid against the practice of military archaeology is the theory that participation by archaeologists in military undertakings legitimizes the coalition invasion of Iraq. From my point of view, the legitimization concept fails to recognize that in the United States the military is required to obey the orders of a government selected by civilians. Some critics of military archaeologists talk about just-versus-unjust wars and their willingness to support the military in a just-versus-unjust cause. The US military does not have the luxury of choosing between just and unjust causes. The military goes to war when ordered to by a civilian commander. The legitimization argument also fails if tested by the concept of the greater good. First, even if every one of the several hundred archaeologists employed by the US military had resigned in protest, it would have had no effect on implementation of military action ordered by a civilian government or on anyone's perception of US military action. The only public reaction I can think of to a mass resignation would be amazement that the DOD had so many archaeologists.

If we consider the greater good, it is important to consider what military archaeologists might be able to accomplish if they continue to work within the system. When the current conflict is over, one of the best hopes for many regions of Iraq is going to be renewal of systematic investigations of ancient Mesopotamian archaeological sites and development of a tourist industry similar to the one driving a major portion of the Egyptian economy. An important contribution military archaeologists can make is education designed to prevent unnecessary impacts on these valuable properties. Our efforts are actually beginning to save sites.[4] It is difficult to see how the participation of archaeologists in planning for and teaching members of the military about the protection of cultural property legitimizes or changes anyone's perception of the nature of civilian-directed US military action in any way.

In September 2008 the US Senate ratified the Hague Convention for the Protection of Cultural Property during Times of Armed Conflict. In taking this action, the civilian government has decided that the US military will endeavor to meet the protocols as defined. These responsibilities specify in chapter 1, article 7 that signatories will "foster in the members of the armed forces a spirit of respect for the culture and cultural property of all peoples."[5] Fostering this respect requires education and training, and when the cultural property in question is archaeological in nature, it is optimal for archaeologists to be the ones providing the necessary expertise.

As I work with soldiers who have returned from deployment, their accounts make it clear that in asymmetric warfare, it is common for insurgents to attempt to strategically use cultural property as firing and cache positions. As US personnel prepare to deploy, they are becoming increasingly aware of the importance of archaeological property and sacred places, and they are requesting more and more cultural information. Many highly principled individuals in uniform intuitively consider sacred and significant property issues when returning fire, sometimes putting themselves at risk. I have had soldiers ask me if it is all right to return fire when—not if—they are being fired on from Muslim cemeteries. This laudable concern is one reason people who fight Americans select cultural properties as fighting positions.

In November 2008 all US citizens had the opportunity to cast a vote in a most historic election. In addition to the privilege of voting, many of us experience other benefits of US citizenship. Many of us live in safe places and are members of communities with social order and sound infrastructure. As I enjoy the privileges of citizenship, I cannot imagine refusing to answer questions or provide information for military personnel who are willing to spend months away from their families, live and work in dangerous places sometimes under miserable conditions, and risk their lives to defend my way of life. To fail to share my expertise, when it is requested in this capacity, would be unethical in the extreme.

An Anthropologist/Archaeologist in a Military Culture

The vast majority of people in uniform I work with have earned my utmost respect, and that respect has increased proportionately with the intensity and frequency of my personal interaction with them. It has been my experience that members of the academic community who are most critical of the US armed forces have the least firsthand experience working with them. Some of the outspoken critics may never have had a conversation with a person wearing a US military uniform. On one occasion, an eminent scholar asked me if US military personnel could read and write. I wish this individual could meet the Marine Corps colonel in Fallujah who briefed his personnel daily and accurately about the history of Mesopotamia.

Now that the DOD has offered me the opportunity to travel into the Middle East with military personnel, I have been able to witness their enthusiasm for learning about other cultures and their appreciation for archaeology, ancient places, and cultural features in the landscape. During my participation at the Eagle Resolve exercises in Abu Dhabi, I inquired about using some unexpected time off to travel to Al Ain, an oasis town on the Oman border that is known for its archaeological sites. Before I could complete the question, a van and driver had been arranged and two high-ranking officers had asked to join me. What followed was a thoroughly enjoyable day where, in addition to seeing archaeology, we were the only Westerners at the goat market and Bedouin tent maker's shops. The officers had many excellent questions, and it was not my only experience being in military company that felt somewhat like defending a dissertation, but in a good way.

It is sometimes easy to forget that military operations include humanitarian relief and nation building. I have worked for officers who airlifted food and water to the Kurds after the first Gulf War, who built schools and infrastructure throughout Africa, and who mobilized as part of the stabilization forces in the Balkans. One of the colonels I know the best spent more than half of his only son's early childhood overseas. A combat-hardened veteran, after months of patiently earning the acceptance of the child who viewed him as a stranger, he sobbed the first time his son invited him to play catch in the front yard. As a young major, this colonel risked being court-martialed to put an injured Somali girl on a helicopter. Her arm was broken, and when the major encountered the situation, local personnel were about to amputate. The transport he arranged saved the child's arm and perhaps her life at the risk of the career he had sacrificed so much for. Ethical behavior ultimately is up to individuals no matter what organization they may belong to or work for. This same colonel called me into his office during the crisis surrounding the horrific behavior of some US military personnel at Abu Ghraib. He explained to me that he was struggling to understand how these abuses had happened. After twenty-six years of service, his anguish was clear, and his comment to me was, "This is not the Army that I serve."

Working for honorable causes from within an organization you may or not agree with often offers opportunities for positive and effective accomplishments that would be difficult to achieve in any other way. As the reader has already concluded, my personal opinion is that the US Army is overall an honorable organization. However, I do clearly understand that I work for an organization that teaches people to use weapons to kill other people. So is it possible to be a person of honor working for a greater good within this framework? My answer is absolutely yes. This answer is supported by examples throughout history in which honorable individuals who were associated with truly evil organizations saved lives and accomplished miracles.

Considering these issues is challenging. There are times when I envy the critics who appear to be able to merely glance at and sign a petition that proclaims their moral high ground as they promise they will never cooperate with the military in any way. As I write this chapter, I'm reminded of the television channel Comedy Central, which features a popular comedian named Stephen Colbert. For me, considering the ethical questions associated with working for the military is an internal version of the episodes in which Colbert puts on a red necktie and then a blue necktie and then debates himself. His sketch is called "Formidable Opponent." I debate myself continuously, and my adolescent children offer some of the toughest questions: Could you work for a commander in chief you didn't respect? Would you shake his hand? Should I ever reach a point where the internal debate ends or seems resolved, it would definitely be time for me to leave the Army.

The military is an organization with strong traditions and appreciation for its heritage. The archaeologist and combat commander find common ground in this regard. Military ceremonies are designed to remind all participants and spectators alike that they are part of a noble organization with a proud history. Uniforms, patches, and flags are symbols that unify the members of each unit within the larger group. The reward system is designed to motivate active duty and civilian employees with actual military medals and coins that can be awarded to a civilian who has been recognized for an exemplary accomplishment or behavior. As a recipient of medals and coins, and as a person who has attended many ceremonies, I can attest that military acculturation is very effective.

The value of my training as an anthropologist is that I have some awareness of how these practices and symbols have worked to make me feel like a valuable part of the organization. As an anthropologist, I also have an ability to view these effects on me from an analytical perspective. I would like to think that this perspective would be advantageous should I encounter a situation in which I would need to objectively separate myself from the organization.

When going to work for the military, I have found training as an anthropologist to be extremely valuable in helping to figure out military culture, a skill required to be effective in a military installation setting. A civilian working in a conservation capacity for the US military has an even more challenging task, because in this context, land management strategies must be compatible with the military mission. The opportunity to develop these strategies is challenging but also very rewarding. The civilian subject matter expert has to remember that the garrison or installation commander is the ultimate decision maker. That being said, the subject matter expert has the opportunity to provide military leaders with all the information and recommendations they need to make sound decisions. A military archaeologist has the opportunity for great accomplishment in the area of heritage preservation.

Military Values

The DOD views itself as a values-based system and is very forthcoming about articulating these values. Many meeting rooms and buildings around Fort Drum have posters featuring the seven Army values: personal courage, honesty, integrity, selfless service, loyalty, duty, and respect. If I were to generalize, I have found that the ethics as expressed by the behavior of the individuals I work with in the Army on a day-to-day basis meet higher ethical standards than the behaviors and events I experienced and witnessed while studying and working in the university setting.

I have also found that in the Army system, it is possible to take an issue, including an incidence of unethical behavior, as high as necessary in the chain of command until it is resolved. On one occasion, I took an issue of supervisory harassment up the chain of command as far as the Pentagon and achieved success. This experience contrasts with my personal experience in university environments where I have found that academic employees often fail to take responsibility or any form of positive action when unethical behavior has occurred. I have seen them lie to their colleagues, abuse powerless students, and take advantage of untenured faculty members. When evidence is brought before committees or ranking administrators, I have yet to encounter a situation that was handled honorably. In contrast, I have discovered that working in an environment where values are defined and articulated on a regular basis causes many employees to at least think about their own behaviors and beliefs in a structured way. I know I find myself considering the Army values in my personal decision-making process. After over thirty years of association with academia, the fall of 2008 marked the first time I ever saw institutional values visibly displayed at a major state university, but when I returned to the university's website to reproduce the list here, I could not find it.[6]

One of the questions raised is whether it is ethical to care about heritage property in war zones where people are being killed and injured. During an interview with the Canadian Broadcasting Corporation program *As It Happens*, presenter Carol Off asked me how I could care about archaeology in Iraq when "children are being killed." My response was that as an archaeologist, I believed the only issue where my expertise could ever benefit the Iraqi people would be in the area of heritage preservation. If one were to attempt to take the argument that concern about archaeology in a war zone is unethical to its not so logical conclusion, all archaeologists should stop working in their areas of interest and join humanitarian organizations that focus on offering medical care and refugee support. I wonder how Off would feel about the Haitians who immediately recognized the need to spare what was left of their museums and historic structures after the January 2010 earthquake and asked the US military to help them. How would she respond to the Italians who expressed the sentiment that for the first time they felt hope for their community after Austrian military cultural property officers rescued sacred objects from their earthquake-ravaged church, enabling them to attend their first Mass after the disaster?

Ethics and Collegial Interaction

The treatment of military archaeologists at the World Archaeology Congress (WAC) in Dublin in 2008 raises the question of a need for ethical guidance in how colleagues in anthropology treat each other. This conference is based on themes, and when the conference announcement was made public, outspoken antiwar activists became chairs of the military and archaeology theme. One of their first decisions was to announce that military archaeologists would not be welcome to present papers in the military-themed session. This decision prompted a lively exchange of views via the Internet. The reason given for banning military personnel was that speakers who were opposed to the war would not feel they could speak freely in front of military colleagues. In the meantime, the DOD had agreed to fund a symposium for the purpose of presenting efforts that military archaeologists were making to address the heritage protection issues in Iraq and Afghanistan. After serious internal conversations among the leadership of the congress, the conference and program chairs felt it was important for the military archaeologists to have a chance to be heard, so they courageously asked us to come and enter our symposia as independent sessions.

In listening to papers in the themed session, I noticed that many of the speakers viewed the US military as an organization that was operating on its own without any guidance from a civilian government. I was embarrassed when a delegate from Austria felt obligated to eloquently remind some of the American speakers about the structure of the US constitutional government. It was also clear that the speakers had no knowledge of US domestic military archaeology inventory, stewardship, and Native American consultation programs.

When we arrived the second day at the designated room for the independent military symposia, we were surprised to see members of the Garda, Ireland's national police service, and university security present. They told us they had been made aware of threats to speakers and were there to provide protection. The Garda had even developed an evacuation plan for us and had brought a special vehicle for that purpose. As a precaution, the security personnel would not let anyone bring hot liquids into the room and may have inspected some bags. Fortunately, the symposia went off smoothly. The only disruption was an American colleague who stepped into the doorway of the room and shouted, "There is no free speech here." We also heard later that some of the individuals who wished to attend the symposia were harassed in the hallway as they approached the room.

The "no free speech" comment made no sense to me until someone explained that rumors were flying around the conference that I had used my "military power" to bring in the Garda to prevent my colleagues from disagreeing with our speakers. I also heard criticism of the military speakers for not wearing their uniforms so they could "blend in" with the "real" archaeologists. I was wearing a variation of my uniform, which is, of course, civilian clothing. After the conference, the president of the congress spent a considerable amount of time tracking down the facts of the matter and wrote a chronology of how the Garda came to be called in. During the course of the conference, petitions expressing opposition to a potential invasion of Iran and pledging not to help the military in any way were passed around for signatures.

The experience of the military archaeologists at the World Archaeology Congress offers a list of behavioral questions, some of them ethical ones. Is it ethical to attempt to censure an opposing point of view at an academic meeting? Is it ethical to harass individuals who want to hear a point of view that is different from one's own? Is it ethical to make up one's own version of events and attempt to pass this version off as fact? Do colleagues have an ethical obligation to learn about a colleague's activity, job, or organization before they declare this colleague to be behaving in an unethical way? And last, what is accomplished when colleagues behave in disruptive ways in the public forum at a scientific meeting?

I hope my antiwar colleagues engage in their own versions of Stephen Colbert's "Formidable Opponent" debate and that I am wrong about the apparent ease with which they sign their petitions. I also feel it is very important that they analyze the effects of university culture on their thinking. There is no doubt in my mind that being in a position of power over undergraduates who profess agreement with you on a daily basis may be just as influential as military ceremonies are on me.

Partnership and the Archaeological Institute of America

In contrast to the behavior of many anthropologists, members of the Archaeological Institute of America (AIA) came forward from the beginning of public awareness of US intentions to invade Iraq in 2003. MacGuire Gibson of the University of Chicago provided site coordinate information to the Pentagon, and these data formed the basis for an Air Force no strike list. The president of the AIA, Brian Rose, became an outspoken advocate for educating members of the military about the archaeology and heritage of the lands where they were headed. He has personally given dozens of lectures and presentations to deploying personnel, some for US Army Civil Affairs and Psychological Operations Command units in cooperation with the US Committee of the Blue Shield, an organization designed to advocate for cultural property protection in the United States. Since 2007 the AIA has been working in partnership with the DOD heritage preservation initiatives to support military education in every possible capacity, in addition to offering archaeological expertise to military personnel with questions. DOD archaeologists have been welcomed at AIA annual meetings, their panels and presentations have been well attended, and the discourse and discussions have been collegial and productive. Although it is beyond the scope of this chapter, an analysis of the nature and origin of the differences between archaeologists trained as anthropologists, as are some of the individuals whom we encountered at the World Archaeology Congress, and archaeologists trained as classicists and art historians, who represent the essence of the AIA, would be fascinating.

Military Anthropologists and Anthropology as a Profession

The year I earned my PhD, anthropology had the distinction of being the academic discipline with the fewest jobs available of all the disciplines. There were very few academic jobs advertised nationwide that year. Even with or maybe because of the tight job market, the notion has persisted within the discipline of anthropology that the only reason an anthropologist would choose to work outside an academic community would be if that individual failed to build a career as a member of a university faculty. In actuality, many of us with outstanding qualifications and training have found more satisfaction in alternative settings and enjoy applying our training in anthropology to real-world challenges on a daily basis.

I view the ethical challenges currently facing anthropology as a threat to the discipline. First of all, when colleagues fail to treat each other with dignity and respect, it sets a poor example for students and encourages them to consider alternatives. If all nonacademic career options within a discipline are presented as being second rate or unethical, what should a student's aspirations be? What is the point of taking the classes or selecting anthropology as a major? What would be the point of a discipline whose only purpose is to train students to become faculty to train more students? Where would the potential contribution to society occur? All forms of human organizations are flawed—even universities. If anthropologists declare the military to be an unethical employer, where would the discipline draw the line? Banks, insurance companies, advertising agencies, manufacturers, and industry? All professions and organizations have aspects that result in the unethical treatment of living beings. If anthropologists disengage from every human organization they do not approve of, who will analyze the structures and values that are generating the unacceptable behaviors? How will meaningful change be effected? Have anthropologists forgotten that individuals can and often do make sound ethical decisions within flawed organizations?

Is it ethical for an individual who was educated at government expense to deny requests for expertise and information to selected groups of students? How should anthropologists choose which students are "worthy"? Why would it be ethical to deny information to young soldiers who want to learn as much as they can about other cultures because they know that misinterpreted hand signals caused deaths at military check points in Iraq? Why would it be acceptable to share identical information with a group of undergraduates who need the same information to successfully fill in the bubbles on multiple-choice answer sheets?

Anthropologists who continue to marginalize the discipline under the guise of ethical decision making are going to find that many practical and gifted students will be drawn to alternative social sciences, like sociology, political science, and international relations. If as a result students are driven to select alternatives to anthropology, the discipline will suffer in at least two ways. First, the rigor students experience in their anthropological cross-culture requirements will be lost. Second, if students eschew anthropology courses in favor of classes from other disciplines, the inevitable consequence will be that funding for new anthropology faculty members will disappear as the alternative departments grow.

Where the Path Is Leading

In terms of progress in the arena of heritage preservation during global military operations, the path that began for me in the old World War II office building has become extraordinary and productive. From a project that created playing cards and websites to teach US soldiers about the archaeology of Iraq and Afghanistan, our efforts have evolved into international initiatives to work in partnership on cultural property preservation issues. We have learned that global military operations in response to natural disasters need cultural property planning information, awareness, and expertise just as badly as activities in conflict zones. In addition to having the opportunity to educate US military leaders about the archaeology of the Middle East in Abu Dhabi, a committed group of colleagues moved forward to establish the Central Command Historical Cultural Action Group with the inevitable abbreviation CHCAG. That group developed the regulatory guidelines for stewardship during *contingency operations*, which is DOD's official term for US military engagement in Iraq and Afghanistan. These guidelines were signed by the central command chief of staff and provide the regulatory enforcement needed to convince military leaders that site preservation is no longer just "nice to do."

The CHCAG, with financial support from the Office of the Secretary of Defense Legacy Program and the Defense Environmental International Cooperation Program, has gone on to provide on-site training in Egypt with the support of Zahi Hawass, secretary-general of the Supreme Council of Egyptian Antiquities during the Bright Star war games. The Bright Star experience and the critical participation of the Netherlands' cultural property officer, Lieutenant Colonel Joris Kila, taught us that international cooperation is critical. We were also fortunate to have participation from cultural resource managers in the United Kingdom, and as a result, the International Military Cultural

Resources Working Group was established in August 2009. Representatives from more than a dozen countries have already expressed interest in the activities of this informal organization that strives to build partnerships for more effective military education concerning cultural property issues. One of its key partnerships is with the Association of National Committees of the Blue Shield.

These defense initiatives, in cooperation with the State Department, supported my opportunity to serve as the military liaison for returning the ancient City of Ur from US stewardship to the Iraqi people. Saddam Hussein constructed military bases on or adjacent to ancient Mesopotamian archaeological sites with the hope that these proximities would provide protective value for the bases, not the sites. In 2003 the United States assumed control of Tallil Air Base, which Saddam had placed immediately adjacent to the ancient City of Ur. In response to massive looting of archaeological sites in the area, the United States extended the air base fence at Tallil to incorporate the ancient city. Because of this decision, the site was successfully protected. As the region stabilized, the United States became increasingly sensitive to Iraqi concerns about access and stewardship. The United States rebuilt the fence, separating the base from the ancient city, and returned Ur in very good condition to Iraqi stewardship on May 13, 2009. This good news story received almost no media attention as opposed to the damage at Babylon.

In February 2010, the CHCAG supported my trip to Kabul to participate in an environmental *shura* hosted by the US Army Corps of Engineers.[7] This experience gave me an opportunity to share a podium and presentation with Abdul Wasi Ferozi, director general of cultural heritage for Afghanistan. Ferozi has risked his life on multiple occasions to protect Afghan heritage, and there are no words in English that can describe the honor of educating members of the American military in partnership with the personification of personal courage that is Ferozi. My presence in Kabul also provided a chance to advocate for US military funding of heritage conservation projects like salvage archaeology at Mes Aynak and the possible construction of a secure artifact storage facility at the National Museum of Afghanistan. Environmental inspections in Bagram and Kandahar gave me the opportunity to meet courageous individuals who are implementing the central command environmental regulations that specify protection of indigenous cultural property. Sites, sacred places, and historic properties are being recognized and spared as a result of their efforts.

Opportunities for military education have continued on the home front as well, from teaching seven hundred military engineers the types of pottery and features I believe should cause them to halt construction and ask for help in someone else's country, to discussing the significance of heritage and environmental issues for future US operations in Afghanistan with military leaders preparing to assume command. The Air Force is supporting a comprehensive project that is engaging the critical issues of providing the information necessary to plan effectively for the presence of cultural property. This project is also building on the accomplishments of the legacy projects and the CHCAG to continue to work on substantive recommendations for a permanent cultural property program within the DOD. In addition, the American Academy in Rome has chosen to recognize military education efforts as worthy of support. The academy gave me a scholarship to live in Rome to write a military education cultural property curriculum, establish a relationship with NATO Defense College, and work to build cultural property partnerships between international organizations, nongovernmental organizations, and international military representatives.

Conclusion

I have made the personal decision that working for the DOD as an archaeologist is consistent with my personal code of ethics. I am also proud to be serving my country as a civilian military employee during a time of war. My politics and personal opinions about the civilian leadership of the United States do not enter into this determination. The "Formidable Opponent" debates I wage with myself allow the possibility of intense disagreement with civilian policies while recognizing that I have an opportunity for accomplishment, which for me is in the interest of the greater good. It is absolutely critical for everyone engaging in discussions of the military and anthropology to remember that in the United States, the military reports to a civilian government and does not have the luxury of choosing its battles. We as American citizens send these people to war. Upon reflection, after more than ten years of working at Fort Drum, I feel that my association with the US Army has been an extraordinary personal and professional opportunity, and I am a far better human being as a result.

Author's Note

The views expressed in this work are the author's alone and do not represent the position of the US Army or any government organization.

Notes

1. See also our paleomaritime website at www.cemml.colostate.edu/paleo/index.htm and publication funded by the Office of the Secretary of Defense Legacy Resource Management Program.

2. Dennis Stanford is curator of North and South American paleolithic, Asian paleolithic, and western US archaeological collections at the Smithsonian Institution.

3. When the US military established a base in Babylon, it damaged the antiquities that were one of the wonders of the ancient world. See UNESCO, "Final Report on Damage Assessments in Babylon," http://unesdoc.unesco.org/images/0018/001831/183134E.pdf.

4. Cooperation between the Army and the State Department saved the site of Tell Arba'ah Kabiir in September 2008 during the expansion of a patrol base. An informed US Army major stopped construction. In 2009 a similar effort saved a series of sites at Forward Operating Base Hammer, also in Iraq.

5. Convention for the Protection of Cultural Properties in the Event of Armed Conflict with Regulations for the Execution of the Convention 1954. www.icrc.org/IHL.nsf/FULL/400?OpenDocument, ch 1, art. 7.

6. The University of Arkansas displays its values on a wall of the student union.

7. A *shura* is a social institution for consultation in which members of a community meet to discuss and make decisions on issues that are important to them.

2

"Living the Dream"
One Military Anthropologist's Initiation

Clementine Fujimura

Clementine Fujimura's chapter offers insights from an anthropologist who has spent the past fifteen years teaching at a military undergraduate institution: the US Naval Academy. Along with an analysis of the academy, this chapter highlights similarities and differences between her experience and that of colleagues in civilian universities. Fujimura and other anthropologists have been hired by the military for reasons other than their disciplinary pedigree, in this case it was her proficiency in multiple foreign languages. To succeed, however, she found it necessary not only to teach anthropologically but to practice anthropology as well. By learning about her students' rituals and rites of passage, she improved their learning experience and heightened her self-awareness of her own liminal status. While changes in military strategy potentially position anthropologists like Fujimura at the center of a profound transformation, she points out that success is far from guaranteed.

I have always been intrigued by people who view the world in a way I have not contemplated. Having spent at least half my life abroad, I am now convinced that very few people see the world as most US citizens do, or as I do. Much of my childhood in fact was spent in Europe (England, France, and Germany). By the time I returned to the United States, I was well into early adulthood and quickly realized that I had become the Other, the outsider, with a different view of the world. The simple ways my friends overseas communicated differed from how my US friends interacted. Then there was the fact that having just come from a foreign country, I was viewed by American teenagers with suspicion. It was an oddity to have a girl fresh from Europe in the class, and certainly her different experiences needed to be approached carefully. In Europe, I had been the "cool American" who must know all about the cool things like American music and fashion. Even American slang was considered a valuable commodity. After all, youth around the world use American slang to demonstrate their coolness and their connection to American pop culture.[1] Not so with German slang in the United States.

I spent my undergraduate years practicing various colloquialisms and mannerisms to see which worked and which did not. I acted out different stereotypical roles in contexts where people did not know me, from being the nerd to the dumb blond. I threw in the study of Russian to complicate things. These personal social experiments were fun and contributed to my understanding of American youth culture while heightening my curiosity about other societies. To quench this thirst, I enrolled in the University of Chicago's PhD program in cultural anthropology where I was swiftly socialized into yet another culture, the world of academia, with its complex, theoretical, and multilayered language and liberal perspective.

My fieldwork took me to Russia to study the concept of childhood as a structuring principle in investigating the lives of children and the attitudes of adults toward themselves, their children, and national identity (Creuziger 1996). Ultimately it led to research on child abandonment and marginalization (Fujimura 2005). The practice of anthropology has a way of forcing researchers to learn about themselves as well as their subject, and true to this, my work in Russia gave me a new perspective on myself and my relationship with the United States.

By the time I was writing my dissertation, I had developed certain beliefs about the country I was a citizen of—it was a good place to be but not perfect. I had no illusions that supported the United States as a superior nation or that democracy needed to be spread around the world. I still held out for the possibility that a better government might exist beyond our borders and our imagination.

On a more fundamental level, I believed (and still do) in my personal obligation, based on experiences with homeless children and my resulting convictions, to oppose marginalization, human rights abuses, and violence. My work with abandoned children, who through no fault of their own are stigmatized for life, made clear to me the importance of society's standing up for the rights of the innocent and victims of forces beyond their control. At the height of the development of these values, I received a call from my most admirable of mentors, Paul Friedrich, urging me to apply for a position at the US Naval Academy.

The decision to apply and subsequently take a position at the academy did not come easily. I had researched personal accounts of childhood in Russia under Stalin, witnessed the losses experienced in Russia during the Afghanistan war, and as the Gulf War was taking place in 1990, I experienced the panic and helplessness many Russians felt at that time. In no way did I want to be part of a machine that implemented war. That being said, I had also learned over the years that to isolate myself from something I knew little about was not the way to learn more about others or about my own values. I decided that working for a short period at the Naval Academy would only teach me more about a small part of an institution that is the US military. I must confess, though, I was biased in the belief that this stint would in all likelihood legitimize my own beliefs and opinions, which framed the military as single-minded, inflexible, brutish, and fanatical in its conservatism.

Checking In

By the time I arrived at the Naval Academy, it had marginalized the study of languages and largely ignored culture as anthropologists understand it. In 1993 Chinese had been cut, Arabic was not seen as a significant language, and Russian language study was threatened with termination from time to time. Few new faculty positions in the field were open, and so my department announced that to cover the future of the new faculty and the department's teaching capabilities, an applicant should speak three of four languages: German, French, Russian, or Japanese. After an interview that required me to teach sections of classes in German, Russian, and French, and to present my work in all three languages as well as in English, I got the job. While my peers in my department were supportive of my teaching languages and culture, I did not get the same sense from the institution as a whole. I had entered a new world, one that did not thrive, as I had all my life, on learning about differences and fuzzy concepts such as culture. This place was gung ho about unity in spirit, the team, and scientific predictability.

The first time I set foot on the grounds of the US Naval Academy, I was struck by the orderliness in the buildings and landscaping, as well as the neatly positioned missiles and small aircraft placed as one might place art in a museum garden. No matter where I walked, I felt I was being watched by the heads of missiles or by those in uniform as I meandered in my summer dress, accompanied by my mutt (a street dog from Chicago), trying to get a feel for my new home, my new workspace.

Not only were the sights new, but even the sounds surprised me. At the University of Chicago, I remember rushing to class with other students, carelessly bumping into one another, lost in music from Walkmans or in books as we tried to navigate winding paths while reading or immersed in energetic conversations with peers. Walking was frustrated by the lack of straight lines and the unpredictable nature of paths that twist and turn.

At the academy, walking was altogether a different experience. Midshipmen walked with a purpose, often quietly, saluting superiors, always wary of passersby. After all, they were being watched by superiors or by tourists. As one midshipman once remarked, "We live in a fishbowl."

The fishbowl experience was mine that first day on what is called "the yard" (not campus, mind you). I was no longer an indistinguishable graduate student. I was a civilian in a military space. I was a faculty member surrounded not simply by students but by midshipmen, the enlisted, officers, and other civilian academics who constitute roughly half the faculty at the academy.

Although no signs prohibit walking across the yard, I feel that doing it would violate the straight lines. I stay on the path even though it does not lead to where I am going. Reaching my destination takes awkward turns down two more paths. It feels as if the missiles are all pointing at me, and still in my anthropological mind-set of extreme sensitivity to symbols and gender relations, I suddenly feel somewhat exposed and vulnerable; it almost does not matter that I am wearing any clothes at all.

I ask my students and military peers how they felt the first time they set foot on the yard. Some of the responses were, "Anxiety over trying to check in on time"; "Did not notice the missiles at all"; "They take themselves too seriously here, this isn't combat and yet they are so tense about everything"; and "On the outside, in public arenas, the buildings look great, but on the inside they are run down—how typical."

The Terrain

To the outsider, the superficial order and control of nature is striking. Flowers and shrubs get changed regularly, like bed linens, to appeal to the taxpayers' eyes. Midshipmen themselves seem indistinguishable as they march in uniform at noon meal formation in parades. The tactful audience of the parade will only fleetingly notice that under the scorching sun on the field, a number of midshipmen faint, dropping flat on their faces or crumbling at the knees.

An awful sight, it is just a small indication that these are individual humans, each with different levels of tolerance, ability, personality, and experiences. Yet from day one, the notion of the individual is quashed. As the new plebes leave their parents in the yearly ritual ceremony of "I-day" (Induction Day, a rite of transition in which those entering the academy change their status from civilian to plebe), they are run through a series of experiences leading to the production of *the midshipman*.

The landscape of the grounds; the structure of daily life; the repetition of ceremonies, rites of passage, and other rituals; and the value placed on these jump out at any student of culture. Indeed, the Naval Academy and the Navy are an anthropologist's aphrodisiac in terms of research potential. Filled with symbolism, an anthropologist is surrounded by hidden (and more often not-so-hidden) meanings begging to be explored.

Anthropologists have long acknowledged the importance of symbols and rituals in describing the essence of culture. As Robert Rubinstein (2008, 74) writes: "Anthropological work leads repeatedly to the conclusion that our capacity for symbolizing is at the root of our experience as a species. Symbolism saturates human experience; people use symbols in nearly every aspect of their lives." The US Navy, and in particular the Naval Academy, uses symbolism to express to the world and invoke in its members its identity and worldview.

The use of ritual as a context is significant to the Navy as it organizes symbols and behavior through performance, in effect accomplishing the goal of ritual that Rubinstein (2008, 75) lays out for us: "Ritual involves the particular constellation of social arrangements that bring about powerful cognitive and affective results. . . . These effects tune the central nervous systems of ritual participants to help them adopt common cognitive, emotional and action orientations toward the world."

Most notable in the ritual organization of the US Navy and the academy experience are the many moments in which liminal phases in rituals entail another rite "nested within it, duplicating all three stages of ritual structure" (Rubinstein 2008, 75). The Navy is organized on the unofficial principle that ritual is essential to the life and survival of the institution. What is more, depending on your function—officer or enlisted, doctor, lawyer, or even spouse, intelligence officer, pilot, special forces, or submariner—you will go through various rites of passage and ceremonies that will reaffirm your identity in the community and the values the institution stands for.

One way a civilian can become a naval officer is to go through a four-year rite of passage by attending and graduating from the Naval Academy. It is one of a few means of achieving officer status but distinguishes itself as emblematic of the value placed on tradition. In fact, it has been argued that the Naval Academy is not the most effective way to educate and train officers. Reserve Officer Training Corps and Officer Candidate School do a fine job of preparing the naval professional, so why should the country spend money on a Naval Academy education? It boils down to the value placed by many US citizens and academy alumni and alumnae on tradition and the symbolism of the academy. In the summer of 2008 the director of the Vice Admiral James B. Stockdale Center for Ethical Leadership, Colonel Arthur J. Athens, US Marine Corps (Ret.), helped me understand the reason for a US Naval Academy by comparing its purpose to the way Lieutenant General Victor H. Krulak, US Marine Corps (Ret.) in 1984 answered the question, "Why does the United States need a Marine Corps?" in his book *First to Fight*: "While the functions which we discharge must always be done by someone, and while an organization such as ours is the correct one to do it, still, in terms of cold mechanical logic, the United States does not *need* a Marine Corps. However, for good reasons which completely transcend cold logic, the United States *wants* a Marine Corps. Those reasons are strong; they are honest, they are deep-rooted and they are above question or criticism" (1991, xx–xxi).

Similarly, the academy expresses American pride in its Navy. The Naval Academy, a producer of high-quality officers and a space of seeming order and perfection, depicted through its landscape and quality training and education, symbolizes this pride. Whether this education and training is in reality any better than that received through the Reserve Officer Training Corps is debatable, but the academy in its architectural and organizational structure "acts symbolically as a visible demonstration" (Rubinstein 2008, 76) of the US Navy's strength.

Upon taking the oath and pledge to join the Navy and the Naval Academy, midshipmen enter a liminal phase—neither fish nor fowl, that is, neither enlisted nor officer. They take orders from the enlisted as well as from officers. Midshipmen may hold a variety of ranks and identities, thus gaining respect from their peers and civilians. However, they receive similar respect in the Navy only after graduating.

I might add here that the significance of status in the military complicates the position of a civilian faculty member (and even more so that of a female civilian faculty member, not to mention that of a minority civilian faculty member, or the worst—a female minority civilian faculty member teaching a "soft" subject). The complexity of my position became immediately clear during the first semester of teaching. I had been asked in my interview how I felt about teaching a predominantly male population of entirely military-bound students. I had no problem with that, especially since the military context implied a certain amount of decorum. However, I had not thought much about how they might perceive me. I figured they would like the idea of a civilian and even a female professor, if only because it offered a glimpse into the world beyond their walls. I had not anticipated that I was seen as lacking in numerous ways. I had no visible signs of status (midshipmen do not always understand the meaning of a PhD, much less the difference between instructor, assistant professor, associate professor, and professor). Moreover, I was somewhat unfamiliar with much of their world, the structure of their lives and their experiences. Perhaps most significantly, I was teaching nonrequired courses in the humanities and social sciences, that is, the soft sciences, the fuzzy sciences, the easy classes (see Fujimura 2003). My only strength was that I was teaching what is generally regarded as a difficult language, Russian.

I would like to return to the notion of the duplication of ritual structure; for not only is the Naval Academy one big liminal phase but within this liminality is nested a whole other ritual required to graduate. This ritual begins with a summer of indoctrination and extends through the first year, which is not only about being neither fish nor fowl in the Navy, but as fourth class (freshman) or plebe, the student is neither fish nor fowl at the Naval Academy. The first-year student is no longer a complete civilian but is considered as not yet having proven worthy of being a midshipman either. The student is one of many plebes, or as they are often referred to by upperclassmen *nasties* or *window-lickers*.

Throughout the summer, plebes are treated separately from the rest of the brigade as they are indoctrinated and go through basic military training and enculturation. If they complete this training successfully, at the end of the summer they are allowed to continue at the academy. During "Reform," when the rest of the brigade returns at the end of the summer, plebes face a year of being rated or tested on the memorization of facts ranging from lists of dishes served at a given meal to trivia about the Navy. While they attend classes, join sports teams, and live with the rest of the brigade, they are still treated as liminal and separate. Even their movement within the dormitory, Bancroft Hall, is different as they must "chop" or turn corners with shouts of "Go Navy!" or "Beat Army!" Throughout the year it is hoped a plebe will acquire the knowledge and attitude to make the transition to the next level—third class—and generally be accepted as a full-fledged midshipman.

This pattern fits neatly into van Gennep's classification of the stages of ritual, described by Rubinstein (2008, 74) during which a member or members are:

1. "separated from general society
2. receive special knowledge that assists their transition to a new life status
3. are reincorporated into society, now in their new status."

After plebe year, midshipmen continue in the rite of becoming officers through more stages similar to those of the first year. Thus, the entire Naval Academy experience can be viewed as one large liminal phase for entering the Navy.

Midshipmen are ranked somewhere between chief petty officer (an enlisted rank) and ensign (an officer rank). During this in-between stage, they learn to become officers. They are incorporated into their institution only upon graduation as new officers.

Understanding the role of ritual and symbolism in the life of a midshipman and an officer became vital to my understanding of my students, my colleagues, my role within the context of the academy, and the full meaning of my work as an anthropologist.

Undercover Anthropology

I had not been hired because of the wonders an anthropologist could do for the academy, but because of the view that my anthropological background might deepen the language training I could offer, and because it suggested a versatility to survive in a department that was under constant threat of elimination. However, while my versatility would help fill gaps as they came up in German, Russian, and potentially even French, my actual education in anthropological theory was not being used. In short, I had been hired by a department that was marginalized, and because I was not a language or literature PhD, the common requirement for entering a language department, I was even more marginal than my departmental peers.

While I understood my assignment was to teach languages, I also understood on a deeper level that language without culture is meaningless, and thus teaching language without teaching culture would be worthless to the students. I felt at home in the language classroom, as students learned not just to translate verbatim, but also to communicate ideas and concepts. Students were open to new ways of looking at the world as they experimented with idioms and turns of phrases, compared translations to texts written by native speakers, and read literature in the native language. Establishing and maintaining a strong summer language immersion program in Russia was a yearly effort, but students returned transformed by their experiences and studies with open minds, enhanced academic and cultural curiosity, and an appreciation for the complexity and respectability of others. As my training and education in anthropology would have led me to predict, the power of the combination of academic rigor and experiential learning was validated. I was applying my knowledge gained in anthropology directly to teaching and felt I had found my niche.

Few midshipmen in the 1990s and the early 2000s were able to take a language because those majoring in engineering and the sciences, which is the majority of students, did not have space in their schedules. Questioning this impossibility fell on deaf ears in the administration, so I redirected my efforts to proposing an introduction to anthropology course that might benefit all midshipmen, allowing them to contemplate in a scholarly fashion the lives of others and the meaning of culture. Unfortunately, not everyone in the administration saw the importance of an anthropological course at the US Naval Academy, as no department offered anthropology. A colleague proposed I simply rename and alter my proposal to make it more palatable to the academy. Since psychology had become an acceptable field of study, I was encouraged to call my course The Psychology of World Cultures and to offer it in a department that taught infrequent psychology courses, the Department of Leadership, Ethics, and Law (LEL).

Generally affiliated with professional development as opposed to academia, LEL comprised mostly military officers who were assigned to teach for a few years. I soon learned the importance of substantiating the contents of my courses to my peers and students. I felt the need to define *anthropology* and its value to future officers in and outside class. I became a teacher not only of students but also of my coworkers and the administrators I took my orders from, with mixed results. While most could not deny the importance of studying culture, few were willing to make room for another course in the curriculum.

Beyond administrative struggles, there were deeper concerns. My assumptions as a new faculty member were flawed on many grounds, the first and most fundamental one being that I seemed to forget that while teaching culture, I was experiencing culture. I assumed from the start that my students and fellow faculty members came with some basic beliefs and values I had found among my students in Chicago—that culture exists, that exploring culture is a worthy cause, and that it is as equally complex and intriguing as any other subject matter offered in any institution of higher education. From a semiotic perspective, I assumed that we could relate to similar metaphors, laugh at the same jokes, and lament the same problems in politics and society, and that basically we would agree.

From a pedagogical perspective, I assumed my students would be naturally curious about Russia, Germany, and anthropology, and that the lectures, texts, and other sources I gave them not only would quench some of this thirst but would also inspire them to engage in intellectual discussions and individual research. As an academic in a military context, I also believed that I would put a human face on their partners and potential adversaries, that my students would come to see what I saw in the countries they would be deployed or assigned to and where they might fight, and that some would reconsider their superficial perceptions of foreign societies. What I seemed to forget throughout all this was that I had arrived in a new place, that I was not the primary teacher—the military was—and that through our interactions I was being shaped by, and only in a miniscule way shaping, the culture I had entered. Without an acceptance of these facts, my teaching would fail, as it initially did.

Over the following semesters, I learned that the Navy and Naval Academy are similar but also vastly different on many levels. The Naval Academy is not one entity but rather a complicated and multilayered organization, consisting of cocultures competing to survive. These cycles ultimately lead to the graduation of about one thousand naval officers each year, who in turn take on leadership roles in the Navy and potentially the US government. It is a cycle of tradition and change, with multiple forces struggling for dominance. The culture of the Naval Academy is a contested zone, not a static or fixed object. It is constantly being constructed and reconstructed through various communication messages that struggle to remain or become dominant (Moon 2002, 16).

As a teacher, I was obliged to learn more about my students. I began my anthropological research by collecting narratives about the lives of students; spending numerous hours of observation in the dormitory, Bancroft Hall (also known as Mother B); and talking to alumni and alumnae about their memories. The complexity of the culture is such that even after fifteen years of teaching and researching I am still learning more about it at the Naval Academy as it unfolds and develops every day.

Sample Findings of an Undercover Anthropologist

Beyond my experiences and analysis of Naval Academy administration and its relationship to culture and anthropology, my study of student life has been most rewarding. It has opened my eyes to why midshipmen behave the way they do in my classes and has helped my classroom become more rewarding for myself and I hope for my students as well.

To begin, I have discovered two umbrella categories of the culture of midshipmen, which I have named Leadership Culture and Counterculture. In all likelihood, there are many other ways to distinguish midshipmen, but I have found these categories helpful since creating leaders is part of the mission at the US Naval Academy.

According to its mission statement, the Naval Academy seeks to develop midshipmen who are able to "assume the highest responsibilities of command, citizenship and government" (see www.usna.edu/mission.htm). This involves the development of attributes, including "selfless leaders who value diversity and create an ethical command climate through their example of personal integrity and moral courage" and "mentally resilient and physically fit officers, who inspire their team to accomplish the most challenging missions, including leading combat." These attributes are developed in midshipmen from the very beginning, during plebe summer, and through the entire four years via military basic training and enculturation in Bancroft Hall, professional training, and academic course work.

Questioning the means of achieving these attributes and the mission is a strong and active counterculture community. While parts of the counterculture are less controversial and even feed into the leadership culture on many levels, others who are less supported challenge the status quo, and still others seem at times to be in direct confrontation to and in contradiction with the mission.

The US Naval Academy Gospel Choir is one example of a subculture that challenges the stereotypes of the Naval Academy but simultaneously feeds into the leadership culture being developed today. As the Navy is acknowledging a need to diversify, the Gospel Choir, which is racially diverse, challenges what it means to sing for Navy and supports the new ideal of diversity. Unlike the more traditionally accepted (and funded) Glee Club, the Gospel Choir does not sing the Navy repertoire, does not stand in a structured fashion, and does not rely on the written words. Rather, the Gospel Choir moves, sings from the soul, and challenges the military structure while representing the newly supported variety of backgrounds the Naval Academy is now courting.

Groups that test and question the leadership culture are the opposite extreme. One such group is the Navy LAX Hooligans, whose members describe themselves as a group of lacrosse fans whose goal is to support the Navy lacrosse team and to enjoy the adrenaline rush and "sense of machismo that comes from being in 'the pit.'"[2] The group considers itself exclusive and will not accept midshipmen who are afraid to challenge the rules of the academy. The members are also exclusive in their homogeneity: white male athletes who participate in contact sports. While they do not proactively try to change the academy, they enjoy challenging rules, and as one member states: "They are letting their actions speak for themselves, and they are indirectly showing the rest of the midshipmen that it is okay to challenge authority and take back some personal freedoms."

The restrictee community is another subculture that thrives in its opposition to the mainstream Naval Academy. It is made up of midshipmen who have been restricted in their freedom because of offenses such as, but certainly not limited to, skipping classes, staying out beyond the allowed time, or worse, having been caught drinking either because they are underage or they drank too much. Often restrictees feel they have been unduly punished. Perceiving themselves as victims, they may bond as a group in opposition to the administration. Depending on the year, this subculture can be quite strong with its traditions and codes of communication. In the 1990s, the restrictee community prided itself on a ritual they started of contributing to the extremely large tape ball, a symbol of the amount of lint those on restriction had to rid themselves of for their numerous uniform inspections. Once the ball became too large, it was started again. Eventually, the ball was confiscated for good by the leadership.

Somewhere in between these groups are those who challenge the system but whose actions are condoned by the administration. One example is the theater group called the Masqueraders. Since its beginning in 1845, this group's existence has been tenuous, depending on funding and official support by the academy. Students join this group "to be in a unique place that is so rigidly uniform." As one midshipman said, "We're vigilantes for creativity, for originality . . . for personality . . . but we also believe that being in the Masqueraders will make you a better officer and better leader. The two don't have to be at odds." Unlike groups that are completely supported or completely unsupported, the support the Masqueraders receive from the academy varies, as the Masqueraders often challenge the audience and Naval Academy community to see the world from different perspectives. The Masqueraders pride themselves on being different from average midshipmen. As one points out, "You can go outside the walls of the Naval Academy and any time you see a midshipman, you can instantly recognize him as a midshipman. . . . Masqueraders you can't pick out." Most important to the group is their fundamental value of the individual and a shared belief in the power of theater to influence and even transform the audience.

The US Naval Academy has not always valued the Masqueraders and has ranked them as a low priority for funding. Outside the classroom, the academy has worked to train and shape military officers with little (and some would argue hardly any) value placed on unique and individualistic input. The Masqueraders offers one venue where individualism and opinion can shine. A new emphasis on embracing diversity will in all likelihood clash with a more traditional value placed on uniformity. The need for further research on contesting values is clear.

While much of my research aids me in becoming a better teacher to midshipmen, some of my work helps those in the institution learn more about it. My research in 2008 resulted in the finding that much of what goes on during plebe summer training sends a message to plebes that is the exact opposite of what is intended by the leadership. The emphasis on diversity may lead midshipmen to believe individuality is valued at the Naval Academy but they will quickly discover during plebe summer that standing out can be a negative characteristic, one that may even get them into trouble. As I heard one detailer (a midshipman who trains plebes) yell, "So you think you are special? So you think we should treat you differently?!" While superficially, diversity is being supported and reflected in the campaign to recruit minorities and women, the traditional training midshipmen receive does not allow for much expression of such differences. Researching similar contradictions between the official line and the true midshipman experience may help the Naval Academy on its way to fulfilling new goals.

The Nature and Importance of Military Anthropology

Despite my initial biases and misgivings, from the beginning of my career I felt lucky to have landed at the academy. At first I thought I was, like beginning midshipmen, "living the dream," a phrase midshipmen use in various ways, depending on the context they find themselves in. Like a plebe entering the academy, I felt honored to have been allowed to become a part of the community, especially since to me it had seemed a closed community, unwilling to engage with the more liberal-minded social scientists. As I continued my journey through the years, I began to understand the more sarcastic connotation of living the dream. For midshipmen, the phrase takes on a less positive tone, as in, "Oh, yeah, I'm living the American dream, one credit at a time!" In other words, the academy they inhabit is an illusion, not the dream they had envisioned before entering.

In the same way that those entering the academy may imagine an idealized experience that does not conform to reality, I had a similar rude awakening. And yet, the reality of the environment became something I felt not only the ability to work with but the necessity to do so. I saw it as an opportunity for anthropology to be useful beyond the anthropological community, to reach a new audience of Americans, and to bring back to anthropology a perspective on our military we had not necessarily seen before.

As anthropologists we often excel in finding meaning in otherness and fail to find the exotic in our own. By approaching subcultures of our own societies critically rather than as we might a foreign culture, we separate ourselves from our own society, thus offering little hope for rich, detailed observation and description we are otherwise so good at: finding fodder allowing for further analysis. Such has been the case with our approach to our own military. Military anthropology offers insight into an American institution that can be viewed as one might another, yet, simultaneously, a highly meaningful part of who we are as Americans. The way the military creates meaning in everyday life and at work has evolved through time and within our midst. As the civilian world has become more separate from the military world, the military has become an island in our midst, one that begs discovering once again. It is at the same time a part of and separate from the United States.

At the academy, my work became more than simply that of a teacher and researcher. I became a military anthropologist whose work included the study of military culture to enable my ability to teach effectively, to inform the military of the cultural dynamics that motivate behavior, and to inform a broader civilian audience about the nature of military culture.

As an anthropologist in a military setting, one cannot help but do anthropology. Even in a regular university setting, some anthropologists are compelled to do the same. Small (2008, 1–2) said, "So what does an anthropologist do when people seem 'alien' to them? It occurred to me that I should enlist the same participant-observation skills I had used successfully my entire career to understand immigration and Tongan culture."

While participant-observation in a military academy is somewhat more complicated than at a civilian university, it can be done. Opportunities such as "midshipman for a day," class field trips, dining with midshipmen, participating in overseas programs with students, and the like have yielded much fieldwork material, as has the permission to observe plebe summer training. As the Naval Academy faces social challenges that have at times concerned the American population, support from within the institution for research that will help honor the mission of the Naval Academy has been strong. Anthropologists have become a valuable commodity to the military as an institution itself, as it seeks to support diversity and enhance communication among ranks, genders, and ethnicities.

Indeed, the role of anthropology in the military is important on many levels. Until now, anthropology has been denied a significant place in the education of military professionals. However, because of the need expressed by the Chief of Naval Operations' (2007, 1) "Language Skills, Regional Expertise and Cultural Awareness Strategy," the study of culture is now seen as vital to the success of the Navy: "Success in achieving the Navy's global strategy depends in large part on our ability to communicate with and comprehend potential adversaries, enduring allies, and emerging partner nations."

Navy officials have realized it is not simply about understanding our enemy, but about understanding our allies to avoid future bloodshed and to aid in peacekeeping operations. The strategy makes clear that the Navy's goal is now to "Implement Building Partner Capacity initiatives (including cultural awareness/language capabilities). Build support for the new Maritime Strategy to include national and international partnerships as elements of Global Maritime Partnerships. Increase and deploy Humanitarian Assistance/Disaster Relief capacities" (Chief of Naval Operations 2007, 4).

Some officers have called this new phenomenon of educating officers to be culturally competent a change in Navy culture and the work of the Navy. Unfortunately, this eagerness to integrate culture into various levels of training and education has not been entirely a coordinated effort, and the fear of those of us who are anthropologists working in the system is that our field will not be taught well enough. Because of a lack of anthropology as a traditional part of military education, other fields are taking on the role of teaching culture to the detriment of the field of anthropology, as culture is presented mostly in textbook fashion rather than as the ever-changing and highly subtle concept it has been discovered to be through anthropology.

This is especially true in training, where military professionals need quick facts for immediate use. As a result, instructors with little training in the field of anthropology themselves, have superficially introduced students to the bare facts necessary for survival or have attempted to teach without a clear understanding of the best way to present cultural studies to a military audience. The emphasis on including culture as part of training (immediate, superficial, and reactive), rather than education (long term, rigorous, and thoughtful), is a problem. Treating culture as anything other than what it is—complex—could be detrimental to anthropology's usefulness and ultimately to the field of anthropology itself.

Notes

1. For more information on the global spread of American slang, see research conducted by Jannis Androutsopoulos, 2005, at www.pbs.org/speak/ahead/globalamerican/slang/.

2. All quotations from midshipmen are from my field notes.

3

A Day in the Life of the Marine Corps Professor of Operational Culture

Paula Holmes-Eber

Paula Holmes-Eber's chapter begins with an experiential account of life as a professor at Marine Corps University. The second section directly addresses how she made the decision to work with the military. While the work of all the contributors has been affected in some way by the events that followed the September 11, 2001, attacks on the United States, Holmes-Eber's trajectory is notable in that her decision to work with the military is more tightly linked to those events than most. In the juxtaposition of the sections, readers will find not only an account of history and choice but also snapshots of how these inform her current work with Marines and civilians. The chapter also illustrates how she has interacted with military colleagues and students with regard to her decisions and current debates in the discipline.

0530

The alarm shatters my sleep. It's dark outside, and I wrap the covers tightly around my head as my husband fumbles for the light. I know that by the time I get to work, I will find several e-mails in my inbox written by Marines who are already in the office at this hour. But, I'm not a Marine.

I rub my eyes and dream wistfully, for a moment, of classes that begin at the civilized time of 10:00 a.m. But that was five years ago when I taught Anthropology of the Middle East and Islam at the Jackson School of

International Studies at the University of Washington in Seattle. Now I teach such oddly named classes as Operational Culture for Strategists or Culture and Small Wars at the Marine Corps University in Quantico, Virginia. And these classes start at 0800. Sharp.

"I'll get us coffee," my husband, Lorenz, says, and pats my arm and pushes back the covers.

"Mmmm," I mumble drowsily and snuggle down into the blankets pretending I don't work on military time.

Not for the first time, I wonder whatever inspired me to take a job as professor of operational culture for the Marine Corps.

0630

"Don't forget your sneakers," I call out to my daughter Yvonne, who is running frantically around the hallway clutching her school bag, her gym bag, a half-eaten bagel, and a dangling sweater. I tuck the shoes into the crook of her arm, and off she races to the bus, legs akimbo, long blonde hair flying.

I hang my pannier on my bike, turn on the flashing red light in the back and the white halogen in the front, and tighten my helmet. I shiver in the cold of the dark early morning. This is always the hard moment: convincing myself to get on my bicycle before dawn. But I know that once I'm pumping away, heat moving down toward my frozen fingers, I'll forget the pain and the cold. There's nothing like pedaling through a Virginia sunrise, sky growing rosy peach above the Potomac River, trees glowing amber and russet and gold in the morning light.

I'm a bicycle addict. And I suspect that's part of the reason the Marine Corps hired me. Strangely, we have some things in common. We both value endurance, persistence, the ability to withstand hardship, and commitment to impossible causes. Like me, many Marines share a love of travel and adventure and a crazy idealistic belief that we have an obligation to do our part for the greater social good.

From May 2003 to August 2004 my husband, my two daughters, and I cycled around the world: 14,932 kilometers, 468 days, across twenty-four countries and four continents to raise $64,000 for asthma research. It doesn't make me a Marine. But at five feet four and a half inches, standing in front of a classroom of thirty-five-year-old Marine majors who have served two, three, or more tours in Iraq and Afghanistan, I'll take any credit I can get.

When I returned from our cycling odyssey, my world had shifted. I was restless. My life seemed pedestrian, pedantic, self-centered. Did my classes on

Islam at the University of Washington really have any impact on the US war in Iraq? Was my latest article on hospitality in North Africa truly relevant to anyone but my small academic circle?

So I was curious when the deputy director of the Marine Corps Center for Advanced Operational Culture Learning (CAOCL) telephoned me in May 2006. One of my colleagues at the US Naval Academy had given him my name. Since I have a PhD in anthropology from Northwestern University with a focus on Arab and Muslim culture in North Africa, I seemed a good fit for the new position CAOCL was funding at Marine Corps University (MCU): professor of operational culture.

I wasn't so sure, however. I'd never heard of operational culture. I knew nothing about the military. And I was fully aware of what the American Anthropological Association (AAA) said about anthropologists who defected and worked for the evil military machine.

0700

I'm pumping down the packed dirt road behind the Officer Candidates School (OCS) on the Marine Corps base in Quantico. By now I know every pothole, every bump. Ahead is a tan Humvee with two Marines standing guard next to it. I slow down, waiting cautiously. There ahead, I see one, two, six blackened faces, crawling along on the ground in between the trees—Marine officer candidates going through early-morning training exercises.

"Morning, ma'am," one of the guards nods his head politely as I pedal past.

The dirt track spills onto the main road along the Potomac River. Down, up, round, and back up again, my legs are pumping hard past the new brick buildings of OCS on my left. Across the train tracks and past the air strip on my right, I peer through the barbed wire fence to see what's on the landing strip today: two twin rotor CH-46 helicopters, affectionately nicknamed Frogs, and a large C-17 transport plane. In my office later today, I figure I'll hear the helicopters' thud-thudding shaking my walls as the pilots put the helos through training maneuvers.

Up over the hill I swing past a row of nondescript 1940s brick buildings that house the Marine Corps media and printing offices. Farther up the road, I see a platoon of Marines out for their morning PT (physical training). Two Marines stand on the corner and hold up traffic to let the group of men and women run by chanting their jodies (cadences).

"Up in the morning with the rising sun," shouts their leader.

"Up in the morning with the rising sun," his Marines call back in time with their steps.

"I'm gonna run all day 'til the runnin's done."

"I'm gonna run all day 'til the runnin's done," the platoon echoes back as it disappears round the corner.

I swoop down round the curve, past the Gray Research Library. It houses books on military history, warfare techniques, international relations, and two old anthropological texts from the 1950s on culture and personality—an approach long ago forgotten except by the US military, which is still using the anthropology given to them by Ruth Benedict and Victor Barnouw.

I swerve to the right, waving to the officers filing into Breckenridge Hall for classes. I drag my bike in the back door of my basement office. The sign at the door reads Anthropologist. My fellow faculty members have titles on their doors like Special Operations Chair, Professor of Security Studies, and Director of Warfighting. When I first arrived at MCU I tried in vain to get my correct title placed on the door. Yet I'd come in each morning only to find even less appropriate new titles like Culture or Anthropology on the shingle. Finally it occurred to me that the Marine Corps was proud to have an anthropologist. So the title remained—testimony to my strange new role in this even stranger new culture.

Inside my office I park my bike and quickly pop my government card into my computer to check my e-mails. Four new ones have already arrived since six o'clock this morning. Nothing that I can't handle after class, so I grab a suit out of the locker in my office and run off to take a shower.

0800

My School of Advanced Warfighting (SAW) students are already seated around the dark wooden conference table, chatting amiably as I enter the room. On the wall of the room hangs a flag captured from the Viet Cong during the Vietnam War, numerous maps of the world, and several plaques awarded to faculty and staff at the school over the years. The male students sit dressed neatly in their everyday camis—green or tan camouflage shirts and pants, tucked carefully into boots. Hair cut one-centimeter short on top, clothes clean and pressed, and no slouching; it's a very different crowd from the ones I taught at the University of Washington as a visiting scholar or at the University of Wisconsin as an assistant professor of anthropology.

This is no group of teenage kids stumbling into class late with torn jeans and forgotten homework. These are seasoned men and women with two, three, or four tours in Iraq, Afghanistan, the Philippines, Somalia, or Bosnia. They have traveled to more foreign countries than most Americans. Several are conversant in Arabic or Pashto, and most of them know more about Islam than their local hometown journalist in some small town in Iowa or Texas or Mississippi. Many have sat cross-legged in an Iraqi sheikh's tent or at an Afghan tribal *jurga* (assembly), negotiating issues that could mean life or death to the Marines in their units and the people in the local villages.

These officers have no patience for simple answers or theory for theory's sake. Most will be deploying again in a few months. It is inspiring and unnerving to realize that what I teach in my classroom today will be put into practice tomorrow. I am fully aware of the immense responsibility and opportunity I have to influence the way these future leaders of the Marine Corps will evaluate the cultural factors in their next operations.

SAW is an elite master's degree program. Out of an extremely competitive pool of well over 120 highly qualified applicants, twenty-four majors and future lieutenant colonels are selected to attend the one-year master's of military science program. The officers come from all four services—Army, Navy, Air Force, and Marine Corps, with an occasional student from the State Department, FBI, or other agency. Usually one or two students are from foreign allied militaries such as Australia or Canada or France. Many go on to complete highly distinguished military careers.

I love my SAW classes. The students are as "sharp as a saw," extremely well prepared, well read, and highly experienced. In our seminars, they have no qualms about debating, challenging, pressing the issues. I always leave the classes feeling exhilarated.

Today the title of the class is Operational Culture: Algeria. In contrast to a standard ten- or fifteen-week class meeting biweekly for a semester, my operational culture course weaves across the SAW curriculum for the full school year. In September I begin with a couple of seminars laying out the basic concepts of anthropology. Then over the months, as the SAW students analyze different military events around the world, I focus on teaching the cultural aspects of the situations underlying the conflicts.

Over the past two years, I have worked hard with the faculty at MCU to develop courses that fit within the military educational framework. Instead of electing classes on a quarter or semester system, all the officers attend an integrated year-long program composed of alternating thematic blocks. A two- to three-week block on the Huk Rebellion in the Philippines might be followed by a two-week war gaming exercise (a simulated conflict situation) set in fictitious Indolaysia. Faculty members work in teams with each other, coordinating their classes to fit within the larger logic of the entire curriculum.

This concept of shared courses reflects Marine Corps values of teamwork. It is an approach completely alien to the academic world of extreme individualism, from which I come. But then again almost everything I do has required adaptation to this strange new culture. Most days I feel I am conducting fieldwork in a foreign country.

"Today we'll be exploring the concept of malleable identity," I begin, pulling out a blue marker and starting to scribble on the whiteboard. The officers smile. I am now quite good at making PowerPoint briefs—the standard presentation style in the military—but I hate them. I dislike the rigidity of a lecture based on slides; it's like a train that is forced to go down a certain track and stop at scheduled stations. I prefer my classes to be organic, evolving in unexpected directions, exploring new concepts not planned into a slide. Most of my students find my approach refreshing, different, eye opening, once they get over the shock of leaving the first class with a whiteboard scribbled all over with six different-colored markers.

"I'd like us to look at it from three different angles," I am scribbling now. "First, we'll look at the articles on the Berber movement and the question of ethnic identity." I switch my blue pen for red. "Next I'd like us to think about the way that language is used to express and define identity." This time I scribble with a green pen. "And finally, I'd like us to discuss the negotiated and changing role of women in Algeria—the way that gender becomes a symbol for a larger issue: Western versus Islamic identity."

Major Wright (all names are pseudonyms) plunges right in. "I disagree with the article comparing the Palestinian-Israeli conflict with Algeria's independence movement. The ethnic issues in Algeria are significantly different. The Berber issue wasn't important during the war with the French. This Berber movement is a new event."

I nod, delighted with the immediate jump into the critical issues. The class has been studying the Algerian war of independence in my colleagues' seminars. We won't be wasting any time tromping through old ground here.

1000

I dash into my office for a quick break and pull up my e-mails. A pop-up meeting request for a discussion of the RCLF (region, culture, and language familiarization program) at the CAOCL heads the list. I confirm my attendance at 1400. There's a note from the Swedish Defence College thanking me for my presentation at its stability operations planning course in Stockholm. Several e-mails circulate *New York Times* and *Washington Post* articles on the latest developments in Afghanistan. I skim some, print a couple, delete the rest. Next is another e-mail on the AAA's position on the Human Terrain System (HTS).[1] I sigh. No point in responding. I've made my decision. And I still don't understand how teaching courses on Islam, Arab culture, ethnic identity, and cross-cultural negotiations violates any AAA ethical standards.

A couple of important e-mails will require some time to answer. I leave them. I need a cup of coffee before getting back to class.

1030

"Morning, Doc," Lieutenant Colonel Slowenski greets me as I head into SAW conference group B. Students in the SAW program are split between two groups so that classes are small, facilitating quality discussions. As a result, each time I teach at SAW, I have to offer the same seminar twice. That doesn't mean the discussion is the same; on the contrary, my students bring their own varied experience to the classroom, making the debates lively and ever changing.

"Doc, did you see that article about the American Anthro Association criticizing anthropologists who work for the military?" Major Haas tosses the question into the room, as I rifle through my papers to get started. "What do you think?" I look up, not totally surprised. Most of the officers in my classes make a serious effort to stay informed about current events. With Washington, DC, only twenty miles up the street, and many of my students' Marine buddies writing from deployments abroad, the officers in my class often know the news before it hits the papers.

I begin to respond, explaining that the AAA's latest statement was actually aimed at the Army's HTS, a program fraught with practical and ethical challenges. "The problem is that many anthropologists just lump everyone who works for the military into one basket," I respond.

By now this has become a class discussion. Major Harper leans forward, "So, ma'am. Since they hate us so much, what made you decide to come and work for us?"

It's a fair question. Some days I look up from the stack of papers on my desk—papers with such strange-sounding titles as "Strategic Plan for Language Skills, Regional Expertise and Cultural Capabilities 2011–2016" (US Department of Defense 2011); "Training Female Engagement Teams: Framework, Content Development, and Lessons Learned" (Allen, Ladenheim, and Stout 2010); or *"Tribes" and Warlords in Southern Afghanistan: 1980–2005* (Guistozzi and Allah 2006), and I wonder, what indeed am I doing here? How *did* I go from teaching and studying about women's kin and social networks in Tunisia to offering classes and writing books and articles on operational culture for Marines?

I struggle to find a simple answer. Was it giving nonstop lectures to the public about the Arab and Muslim world after September 11, 2001, including televised ones to packed audiences of over three thousand people struggling to make sense of their new world? Was it the realization that despite allowing students to overenroll in my courses Peoples and Cultures of the Middle East or Anthropology of Islam I would have virtually no impact on the unfolding events in Iraq and Afghanistan? Did I suddenly develop a sense of moral responsibility after seeing firsthand the poverty, hunger, and corruption as I pedaled through Russia, China, or Tonga?

I smile and offer my answer. "Well actually, the reason I finally decided to come here was because of a set of Sitreps [site reports] from the Horn of Africa." I pull my hand down from twirling my curly blonde hair—one of those nervous habits that make me so very un-Marine-like.

"After I got the job offer, I debated for a month trying to make a decision. Then the deputy director of CAOCL started faxing me these Sitreps. I couldn't believe it. Marines were inoculating cows. Digging wells. Treating sick kids. And I thought—this can't be the military! Marines kill people." The officers in my classroom are gazing intently at me now. They're being patient with me; they know that civilians—especially academics—hold many uninformed prejudices about the military.

"I realized I didn't have a clue what the military really does. I had no idea that Marines were even in Africa. I thought the only organizations doing things like stability operations or humanitarian affairs were nongovernmental organizations like the Red Cross." I pause, trying to put my thoughts together clearly. "I was surprised that the Marine Corps was genuinely looking for assistance in understanding the cultures of the people in Iraq. They were asking me to help them understand and work with the local people. And it occurred to me—if I didn't step up to do the job, who would?"

The officers around the table settle imperceptibly. A few smile and nod. I appreciate their concern. It's not always been easy teaching here. I mix up acronyms. I make mistakes confusing the different MEUs (Marine expeditionary units) and MEFs (Marine expeditionary forces), and the S-2s and G-3s. I am useless when it comes to military history. But most of them appreciate what I've given up to come here. While they might smile at the way I dance in front of the classroom (in contrast to proper military rigidity), they can't understand why my colleagues and my discipline fail to see what they clearly understand: that my work is far more likely to lead to increased international cultural understanding and peaceful solutions than years of polemic, antagonistic articles in the *New York Times*.

1230

I drop my books and notes onto the desk in my office and collapse, exhausted, into my chair. Absentmindedly munching on a hummus and pita sandwich, I browse through my e-mails. I rarely take a lunch hour, unless I have a visitor who needs entertaining. Q-town, as Quantico, the town on the Marine Corps base, is affectionately called, is a dismal collection of barber shops, abandoned buildings, and greasy hamburger joints—a far cry from the quaint college town of my undergraduate years at Dartmouth or the cosmopolitan life of the Northwestern and University of Washington campuses.

Occasionally I long desperately to call up a friend, meet for lunch at my favorite Pakistani restaurant on the "Ave" in Seattle, and have a long conversation about some totally academic subject like the ritual meaning of women's shrine visitations in Egypt. It's lonely out here. When I arrived at MCU, only one other civilian woman was on the faculty of over sixty professors and chairs.

About 60 percent of the faculty is composed of senior Marine officers who swing through on a two-year tour. With one or two rare exceptions, the civilian faculty is composed of retired military officers who continued on to get a PhD in military history or political science. I am the first anthropology professor MCU has ever hired.

To my delight, Kerry Fosher, a fellow anthropologist, arrived one year after I took my position to work as the command social scientist for the Marine Corps Intelligence Activity and then later as the research director for the culture center, CAOCL. Every now and then we meet at her house to share our projects, discuss our various challenges working for the military, and ponder the true meaning of liminality as we drink coffee and nibble on scones in her living room.

1255

"Afternoon, ma'am."

I smile and look up at Major Castello, who has an appointment at 1300 to discuss his master's thesis with me. Major Castello is one of my students at Command and Staff College (CSC), one of the four colleges at MCU, each with a distinct curriculum designed for the specific rank of its students. The Expeditionary Warfare School is the captains' school. CSC is for the majors, SAW is for majors selected to become lieutenant colonels, and the Marine Corps War College (MCWAR) is for lieutenant colonels. I teach at all four schools, and since each school has its own distinct eight- to eleven-month curriculum, my teaching schedule is erratic and often hard to track. One month SAW moved one of my classes without informing me, and I ended up scheduled to teach Operational Culture: Vietnam at SAW and Operational Culture: The Middle East at CSC at 0800 on the same Tuesday morning.

Major Castello stands politely at attention in the entrance to my doorway. Six feet tall, taut and tanned from years of travel overseas, walking with an almost regal upright grace, Castello would stand out in any American crowd.

"Have a seat," I motion to one of the chairs in my office, pulling out his thesis draft and setting it down on my desk. Despite his height Major Castello bends fluidly into the chair, legs straight and back upright, waiting patiently for me to gather my thoughts. "This is coming along well," I smile, opening the first page. Actually, the paper is outstanding. But I have learned that Marines are uncomfortable with exuberant praise.

"The intro is good," I flip the pages quickly. "And I have a few comments." I point out my scribbles in the margins as Major Castello looks on. "But what I think we really want to work on is the model." I point to the diagram of cultural distance Major Castello has developed. Marines have a strong preference for representing information visually. Major Castello's paper offers a computerized model for representing cultural values in a manner that is intelligible to the military community. "The question is," I ask, "how are you going to measure these cultural values?"

"That's where case studies are necessary," he begins in a soft Spanish lilt. Major Castello's family is Argentinean. He understands on a personal level the challenges of working across cultures. "What I'm thinking is I'd like to use a Middle Eastern country as an example for the various dimensions," he begins, flipping ahead to the next section. Soon I am happily engrossed in a discussion of Middle Eastern and American culture, the challenges of cross-cultural communication in a military environment, and the limitations of computer analysis using qualitative ethnographic data.

1345

Hastily, I wriggle into my North Face jacket, cinching my bicycle helmet around my chin. Packing my laptop computer into my pannier, I wheel my Fisher city touring bike—half mountain-, half road bike—out the back door and hop onto the saddle. I swing right around the Grey Research Library and then left into a muddy potholed parking lot. Within six minutes I'm rolling my bike to the rack in front of a set of double-wide trailers—the home of CAOCL. The Amtrak train lines run behind the trailers, leading to the standard joke at CAOCL that we work in trailers on the wrong side of the tracks. There's more truth to the joke than meets the eye. The Marine Corps' culture venture has not necessarily been accepted by all, as evidenced by the temporary housing CAOCL occupies. Certainly the center's professional image is not enhanced by shouting into our phones, "General, can you hold on for a minute?" as the 1545 train roars on by.

As I open the door to the southern trailer, I am overwhelmed with the scent of saffron and cumin. The Afghan culture and language instructors have just finished their communal lunch of scented rice, lamb stew, and cilantro-laced salad on the shaky wooden table in the back.

"Ahlan ya ustheth (Hello, Professor)," Farid, our Iraqi instructor greets me in Arabic. "Kef alhal? (How are you?)"

"Behir alhamdulillah (Well)," I respond smiling, wending my way to the back among the crowd of desks and hubbub of Arabic, Pashto, Farsi, and French filling the air. If the Horn of Africa Sitreps convinced me that ethically I needed to work for the Marine Corps, CAOCL's vibrant multicultural atmosphere attracted me personally. Each time I step into the culture center's trailers I feel as if I've landed in a lively Middle Eastern souk.

Reaching the back wall of offices, I heave my pannier onto my desk. "Bonjour, Maurice," I call out to my office mate, kissing him on the cheek—left, right, left—according to French custom. Maurice is a retired French Marine colonel with over twenty years of experience conducting military operations from Senegal to Chad to Algeria. He is in charge of creating and teaching courses to US Marines deploying to Africa.

Although CAOCL's main cultural focus today is Iraq and Afghanistan, its goal is to build a curriculum that spans all continents, providing courses on the languages and cultures of Latin America, Africa, the Pacific, South and Southeast Asia, Central Asia, and former Soviet states. One of the unique features of the Marine Corps is that at any given time, Marines can be found deployed all over the world, assisting in disaster relief after a tsunami or hurricane, providing police and military training to partner nations, running rescue missions for stranded American civilians caught in a sudden war or crisis, conducting civil affairs projects such as building roads or medical clinics to provide stability and reconstruction in war-torn countries, as well as, of course, fighting in large- and small-scale wars.

Hurrying, I shrug off my jacket, pull out my journal and a pen, and swing out the door to the region, culture, and language familiarization meeting. RCLF is an ambitious effort to build on this concept of a world cultural education program. CAOCL has been developing a regionally focused culture curriculum splitting the world up into seventeen micro-regions. Ultimately, every career-level Marine will be assigned a region and required to study that region's culture and language via online classes.

The RCLF curriculum has been one of my many projects at CAOCL. In theory I devote 70 percent of my time to the university and 30 percent to the culture center. However until Kerry Fosher joined CAOCL a year ago, I was the sole anthropologist working for two separate organizations, both of which needed a full-time expert on cultural issues. Over the past five years here my work at CAOCL has ranged far and wide: from overseeing the RCLF North Africa course, to creating a Marine Corps operational culture curriculum to be taught at every base to every Marine, to providing instructor development classes to the instructors and curriculum developers, to providing oversight and critique of doctrinal and training materials, to interviewing Marines returning from the field, to designing and running a survey of 2,400 Marines on cultural issues, to participating in Department of Defense culture policy meetings, to visiting with other military culture programs across US military services and as far and wide as the Israeli Military Psychology Center and NATO's senior leadership courses, to writing and publishing books and articles on culture for use in the military classroom. I often feel like I'm balancing a high stack of boxes on a tightrope. As long as I keep moving forward and don't look down, I won't fall.

"Tu viens aussi, Maurice? (Are you coming also, Maurice?)," I ask as I head toward the CAOCL conference room. He smiles and nods as I disappear out the door.

1600

I stare at the dancing *e* on the computer screen in front of me. The secure computer operating system used by the Marine Corps has timed me out as usual. So I type my password back in to log on. I'm back in my office at MCU after a two-hour-long meeting, wading through my e-mails for the day.

I've been trying to compose a polite e-mail commenting on the latest human behavior simulation model. Three days ago I attended a demonstration of a highly entertaining cultural education computer game set in Iraq. Players had to navigate through various cultural scenarios—entering an Iraqi home, walking through a traditional souk, running a checkpoint. To win they had to interact successfully with local people. The designer of the game was an obvious programming wizard. The sheikh in his long robes and turban could have stepped out of a Disney movie. Unfortunately, as with many of the computer models I have seen lately, the sociocultural basis for the Iraqi characters' behavior was limited, to say the least.

I begin to type, "Although the programming is excellent, the scenarios are unrealistic and do not reflect appropriate human behavior." Too polite. Backspace, backspace, backspace. I delete the line and try again. "Models such as these have the allure of highly sophisticated colorful computer games, which appeal to our young Marines who have grown up on Nintendo. However, without the appropriate scientific data to back the behavior of the actors . . ." Too academic. I select and erase again. I've learned that when I get into my professor mode and start speaking academese, all I get are glazed looks.

What I really want to say is, "Hey guys, don't buy the multimillion dollar shiny toy because it looks great. If you look inside, there's no substance, no research to support it." The problem is that the US military loves technology—it adores flashy, shiny products with talking figures and sophisticated imagery. When I try to explain that the cultural information inside the fancy package is based on dubious Google searches and Wikipedia, the typical response is, "What's wrong with Wikipedia?"

1745

I switch off my computer and look longingly at the stack of articles on my desk. Once upon a time in the faraway land of civilian academia, I would sit in my office and read for hours upon end. Now I skim and inhale articles in the same frantic manner as my desk lunches. I begin to pull on my cycling tights, fantasizing about long undisturbed summer days in Seattle when I would read and think and debate and write.

I deliberately avoid looking at the pile of writing projects sitting untouched on the corner of my desk. I have a chapter to write about being an anthropologist for the military, a paper to present on the results of our Marine Corps culture and language survey, and a volume of papers on culture case studies to edit for a forthcoming book. There's always tomorrow, I think hopefully, switching off my light and closing the door as I lean my bike against the hallway wall.

The sun is low in the sky, spreading a hazy crimson along the skyline. Up, down, up, down I push the pedals, breathing sharply in the cold air. Slowly the blood moves out toward my fingers and toes as I gather speed, swinging again past the airstrip—the helicopters are no longer on the tarmac since they're circling in the air, their blades thud-thudding against the reddening sky. Down the hill and over to the OCS, I pass a green line of new recruits moving stiffly along the outdoor dinner table, scooping mashed potatoes and meatballs onto their plates as their drill instructors (DIs) bark orders.

I turn right onto the off-road trails behind OCS. Two neat rows of green domed tents sit on the lawn in between the obstacle course. It's a cold night for camping, I muse. For a moment I pause, gazing at the small fragile domes, their doors flapping in the wind. Why would anybody apply to join the Marine Corps, crawling around on your belly in the early morning dark, testing your leadership through impossible scenarios with DIs constantly shouting in your ears, and spending the night camping in thirty-degree weather, all the while knowing that if you make it you'll soon be shipped off to Afghanistan or the Philippines or the Horn of Africa?

Why would anyone become a professor of operational culture, crawling out of bed before dawn every day, struggling to pronounce impossible acronyms to speak to this strange foreign Marine tribe, and worrying about whether the culture curriculum is accurate while falling asleep at night knowing that many anthropologists believe my work to provide cultural understanding to the military is unethical and unprofessional.

The tunnel of green trees closes in, amber sunlight speckled along the trail. Up, down, up, down, my legs push harder and faster, harder and faster until the trees and the sun and the path blend red and green and brown, beckoning me, calling me to blaze a new trail into unknown territory, into a world where Marines are as likely to build schools as to blow up bridges, treat the gunshot wounds of Iraqi civilians as shoot insurgents, and storm not only the beaches of Tarawa but also the tsunami-struck islands of Indonesia, carrying food and water in humanitarian aid.

Notes on Becoming the Marine Corps Professor of Operational Culture

While each anthropologist who chooses to work for the military has a personal narrative, some themes draw together my own experiences with those of the other contributors to this book. Like the experiences of many of my colleagues, becoming a professor of operational culture has been an unusual and unexpected process filled with challenges and surprises, as well as much career satisfaction.

On Becoming an Anthropologist

Like my other cocontributors in this book, I consider myself to be first and foremost an anthropologist, a scholar who works with people from other cultures, researching and analyzing the way people in different cultures construct their worlds and navigate their social relationships with others. I was attracted to anthropology not because I intended to work for the military; indeed on the contrary, I had absolutely no idea when I began graduate school that my career path would lead me to such a novel and challenging position. My decision to obtain a PhD in anthropology, in fact, was a logical growth of my interest in human behavior combined with my passion for travel, adventure, and the desire to live and work with people whose lives and perspectives were radically different from my own.

Because of my father's work in oil prospecting, my family moved frequently when I was a child. By the time I was fifteen I had lived in eighteen different houses in England, the United States, and Canada, and was fairly competent in speaking and reading French and German as well as English. As an undergraduate at Dartmouth College, I continued my interest in foreign languages and cultures, studying Italian in Florence and taking a life-changing trip to Morocco afterward. My experiences in this exotic Arab country inspired me ultimately to focus on North Africa and Arab and Muslim culture in my graduate studies at Northwestern University.

Like several of the contributors to this book, however, I did not gravitate toward anthropology immediately. My undergraduate major was in psychology and sociology, an education that has given my research and work a strong statistical and quantitative as well as qualitative grounding. As a graduate student in anthropology I became fascinated with the cultural and gendered nature of social networks in Arab society when writing my dissertation and then a book on the subject (Holmes-Eber 2003). Thus began a ten-year-long traditional academic civilian career of researching and teaching about Muslim women, Arab culture, and the family in North Africa and the Middle East. After receiving my PhD, I spent four years as an assistant professor of anthropology at the University of Wisconsin–Milwaukee. My husband and I then moved to Seattle where I continued to teach as a visiting scholar for the Middle East Center at the Jackson School of International Studies at the University of Washington. I found my career satisfying and interesting; it never occurred to me I might one day end up teaching Marines at MCU in Quantico, Virginia.

Then unexpectedly on September 11, 2001, everything changed, and my career was jettisoned into a new direction: working for the military.

On Becoming a Military Anthropologist

Within hours of the attacks on the Pentagon and the twin towers of the World Trade Center, the Middle East Center began receiving a flood of calls: Why was this happening? Who were the perpetrators? Did the center have professors and experts who would be willing to talk to the newspapers, on television or the radio, and give lectures to groups ranging from the Women's League of Voters to being keynote speakers at local college convocations? Without warning, whether or not I wanted it, I and my other colleagues at the Middle East Center were thrust into an unfamiliar world of media, news, and public speaking. Suddenly we were forced to leave our comfortable scholarly offices and address real-life issues, answer questions about public and government policy, and become counselors and advocates in an unfamiliar and changing political environment.

The experience was exhausting. Like most of my colleagues, within three months I had given an average of one guest lecture a week and consulted almost daily for many of the leading newspapers and television programs. The experience was also humbling. For the first time in my life I began to question the relevance of what I did in academia. What was the value of studying the Middle East and Muslim cultures if my research and teaching only advanced my personal status within the ivory tower? Did I have the right to simply sit comfortably on the sidelines as hundreds of thousands of people died, critiquing our government and military for their mistakes without making any effort to improve the situation? Because of these deep fundamental concerns in part, I took a year off to work for a nonprofit organization, cycling around the world with my family to raise money for asthma research (details about this trip can be found at www.worldbikeforbreath.org).

When I returned, it became clear to me that my current career path in academia was no longer fulfilling. I resumed my position at the University of Washington, but somehow I seemed to be going through the motions; my heart was elsewhere, focused on the ongoing political-military drama in the Middle East. I felt strongly that I had a moral obligation to contribute my knowledge and skills to a government that seemed sorely in need of competent expertise on the region. Ultimately, after a rather unexpected opportunity arose to teach at MCU, I accepted the position as professor of operational culture (see Holmes-Eber 2011).

On Becoming a Professor of Operational Culture

Honestly, my work for MCU has not always been easy. As I was the very first professor of operational culture, there have been few precedents, which is a blessing and a curse. In my first year at MCU, I had to develop an entirely new culture curriculum for a military university that had historically taught such courses as The Peloponnesian Wars and Air Power in Vietnam. A few months into my work I realized that thirty-five-year-old Marine majors were not interested in reading introductory anthropology textbooks with pictures of the dance rituals of some exotic peoples on the front cover. As a result I ended up coauthoring a textbook on cultural principles that would appropriately address the needs of a military audience, providing examples that illustrated the cultural principles in contexts the Marines were likely to experience (Salmoni and Holmes-Eber, 2011).

Perhaps the most difficult task, however, was to convince my students and colleagues alike that not only are classes on culture as important as classes on military history, but also that a blonde-haired female civilian with no military background was capable of teaching a classroom of two hundred seasoned Marine majors. Indeed one of my greatest challenges has been realizing that at the same time I was teaching anthropology, I also had to practice it.

I discovered early that I was working in one of the most fascinating foreign cultures of my life—the Marine Corps. Marines speak differently, walk differently, interact differently, and think about their work and life in ways completely foreign to American culture. In my first year of teaching, I suffered from the same symptoms of culture shock I had experienced when I conducted my fieldwork in Tunisia. This culture shock was even more extreme because I did not expect it; I assumed that I was in my own country and that my behavior and ways of approaching the world were understood by my students.

Initially I taught classes in ways the Marines found strange and humorous. While the Marines were patient and polite to me in public, I was devastated to find that behind my back they considered me "that West Coast, hippy, bangle-toting chick." They nicknamed my CSC class "the Riverdance" because I "danced" around the room as I talked, waving my hands excitedly as I discussed the material.

Equally challenging was my work outside the classroom. Coming from a competitive, individualistic academic environment, I was shocked to find that often my work was not my own. As Marines frequently remind each other, "There is no 'I' in Team." I was horrified the first time one of my projects was *murder boarded*. In a one-hour period all my colleagues literally murdered every word and image I had put together in a presentation, rewriting it until they were all satisfied with the outcome.

I reached my lowest point, breaking into tears one year into my new job, after reading a course review that stated, "If Dr. Holmes-Eber is going to teach us about culture, she should take her own lessons and learn about Marine Corps culture first."

So I did. I realized that just as I had had to learn to dress, move about, and interact with men and women differently during my fieldwork in Arab and Muslim cultures, I would also have to understand and adapt to this strange new culture of the military. After carefully observing military professors teach their classes, I learned quickly to use PowerPoint, to move more rigidly, to speak more authoritatively, and to wear the dreaded black Washington, DC suit in the classroom.

Fortunately, my leadership understood the challenges I faced, and we both realized that an extraordinary opportunity lay in front of us. It was clear that I needed to understand the culture of the Marine Corps if I wanted to develop classes and materials that Marines would use. So with the support and guidance of my bosses, over the next four years I conducted an ethnography of Marine Corps culture. I interviewed Marines about their work and their deployments to understand the situations they faced when overseas. I traveled to different Marine Corps bases to observe their training exercises so I could see how and what they learned. And wherever I went, I wrote down acronyms and favorite sayings and would ask Marines to explain them to me. Slowly I began to develop classes that were relevant to my students, and I became more and more competent speaking in ways that made sense to them. Currently I am writing about and publishing this research, providing a unique ethnographic insight into one of the most powerful and yet rarely studied cultural groups in the United States today.

In the process of this fieldwork I found a balance, maintaining my own culture and identity while being able to move comfortably and effectively in the military world. While I do wear suits to meetings and in the classroom, on my nonteaching days in my office I wear my more "anthropological" skirts and dresses. I use PowerPoint in the appropriate settings, but I'm perfectly comfortable with scribbling in multiple colors on a whiteboard if I believe the students will learn better that way. I tend to select a mix of readings, alternating a set of military articles with scholarly anthropological journal articles.

And as for the dancing—well, I can stand stiffly and sternly in front of the classroom and shout out, "Good morning, Marines" to my students, expecting the classic Marine Corps response, "Errr." But then, depending on the context, I still do an occasional anthropology dance when I get excited about the topic.

Conclusion

Certainly my career path is unconventional. And yet much of what I do is still academic anthropology. I teach and prepare courses on cultural principles and cultures of the Middle East, I write and publish scholarly books and articles, and I conduct ethnographic fieldwork. The difference is that at the end of the academic year, my students deploy to the places we have studied in the classroom. Facing difficult conflict situations, they seek to apply the principles they have learned and solve complex cultural problems without necessarily shooting a gun. Seeing my classes translated into positive actions in the field provides a sense of satisfaction and fulfillment that is unparalleled in all of my years of teaching. I do not regret my choice.

Author's Note

The opinions expressed in this chapter are the author's own and do not represent those of the Marine Corps University, the Marine Corps Center for Advanced Operational Culture Learning, the Department of Defense, or the US government.

Note

1. HTS is an Army program described briefly in the introduction to this book. HTS involved placing social scientists of extremely varying educational backgrounds and expertise with Army units deployed in Afghanistan and Iraq. The program received extensive comment and critique by the anthropological community, and the discussion can be followed better elsewhere. Marines had contact with HTS teams and occasionally worked with them when deployed. However, Marines never adopted the program for use by the Corps; it remained an Army function only.

4

The Road Turnley Took

Jessica Glicken Turnley

Jessica Glicken Turnley's chapter captures a long and varied work history that only recently brought her into contact with the military. Turnley fully confronts the reader with the complex personal and intellectual trajectory, historical circumstances, and choices that led her to engage with different aspects of national security institutions. She addresses how earlier choices, graduate training at some of anthropology's elite departments, and work have shaped the kinds of projects she takes on and how she approaches them. She also offers insight into how the part of the military an anthropologist first encounters, in her case special operations, can influence the degree and type of engagement, as well as the way anthropologists and their work are received. This last aspect is particularly important, as the long-term consequences of the point of entrée represent a largely unexplored aspect of anthropological work with the military.

I am a civilian contractor working with the military. More specifically, I own and run a consulting business in Albuquerque, New Mexico, that currently does most of its business with the national security community, and a good deal of that with the military and Department of Defense (DOD). I have come late in my career to this work with the military, and working with the military is not all I do. I believe this diversity in practice is a good part of what I bring to all my clients, including the military. If creativity is making new or nonobvious connections, my variegated career has given me much to connect.

Some definitions might help to contextualize this story, as it is a bit different from others in this volume. The *national security community* is a broad term that goes far beyond the DOD and the military. Historically, until September

11, 2001, the national security community primarily included federal organizations, the private sector, and quasi-public organizations such as Washington, DC think tanks. In short, at one time this was called the military-industrial complex. Federal organizations particularly relevant to me then included the DOD (but not the military services); the Department of Energy with its work in nuclear weapons development conducted through the national laboratories of Los Alamos, Sandia, and Lawrence Livermore (which also do other defense- and energy-related work); and the intelligence community (which includes the Central Intelligence Agency and over a dozen other agencies). The post-9/11 world clearly added the Department of Homeland Security to the list, as well as state, local, and tribal entities.

More interestingly, the post-9/11 national security environment spawned a debate that is still going on about the scope of the national security community. If the threat is really to our way of life, and if our weapons of defense are now recognized to run the gamut from diplomatic to information to military to economic, shouldn't the State Department be on the list? And how about the Department of the Treasury or the Department of Commerce? And since the lines between foreign and domestic are blurred by nonstate actors with few or no geopolitical loyalties, the lines between criminal action and war aren't so clear any more. So, should the Department of Justice and the Federal Bureau of Investigation be part of the national security community? And how do we then deal with the legal, cultural, and ethical questions that arise from blurring these lines? As we challenge the definition and scope of the national security community because of our changed circumstances, some very interesting questions arise with strong anthropological dimensions about the relationship of organizational structure to behavior. These and related questions are all topics I discuss. But I'm getting ahead of myself.

I think it's best to begin my story of engagement with the military from the beginning. As the King of Hearts said to the White Rabbit in Alice's wonderland, "Begin at the beginning, the King said, very gravely, and go on till you come to the end: then stop" (Carroll 1960, 158). And so I shall. This is a story of choices made. My choices took me from a culturally diverse high school to Indonesia, Silicon Valley, Albuquerque, microeconomic development, national security, and nuclear weapons before I ended up with the military. As my road was a crooked one, and as each step along it contributed to my ability to interact the way I do, a good part of this story is about who I am.

The beginning is really high school, the beginning of many things. This was the birth of my interest in anthropology, although I didn't know it by that name then. I went to Venice High School, a Los Angeles public school. We were a minority majority school long before it was fashionable. There were four distinct ethnic populations at the school, then referred to as Blacks, Chicanos, Japanese, and Whites.

The Japanese and the Chicanos particularly interested me. Why did one group (the Chicanos) focus on cars and families, and the other (the Japanese) on academic achievement? They both came from strong ethnic communities, spoke another language as their first, and often had parents who spoke no English at all. So why were our top graduates Japanese (with a smattering of White kids) and the kids in the tutoring programs predominantly Chicano (and Black)? It was my first anthropological question.

I left Venice High and went four hundred miles north to the University of California at Santa Cruz, sprawled among the redwoods on the north side of Monterey Bay. I arrived in 1970. The school had been open only five years, and with only three thousand students, it was smaller than Venice High. There were no grades, just pass/fail, and a narrative evaluation from the professor on your performance. There were no graduate programs when I started, so all faculty focused on undergraduates. It was heaven in the redwoods. You could get a great education or have a great time for four years. It was up to you.

I loved to read and figured I might just as well get credit for it, so I became a literature major and discovered literary criticism. As part of my college exploration, like many others, I took introductory courses in a variety of social and behavioral sciences including anthropology. However, I must admit I never did see the connection between circulating connubial marriage and my questions about my high school compatriots. I decided anthropology wasn't for me and that I would stick with literature.

Then I took a class on language and culture. A whole new world opened up to me. I went back to anthropological theory and discovered Clifford Geertz and thick description and was able to marry my interest in literature with my cultural questions through his interpretive approaches. I declared a double major in anthropology and English literature and attended seminars by Gregory Bateson and Sherry Errington. Roger Keesing supervised my undergraduate thesis on the American cowboy as a cultural icon through the cowboy's depiction in two novels written over seventy-five years apart: Owen Wister's *The Virginian* and James Fenimore Cooper's *The Last of the Mohicans*. I had begun to find a vocabulary for my questions about my high school compatriots and was learning new ways to think about the culture I was embedded in. All the while we were making trips up to San Francisco to hear the Grateful Dead and the Rolling Stones, to peace march the streets of the city, and to wander through the sad alleys of Haight-Ashbury.

After a year off in which I ran a campus coffee shop in Santa Cruz, hung out on the beach, and put seven thousand miles on my bicycle, I went to the University of Michigan at Ann Arbor. Culture shock. I went from a school of three thousand students to a school of forty thousand, from a pass/fail system to a graduate program that overadmitted and used a highly competitive first year to weed out candidates, and from a strongly humanistic approach to anthropology to a department that was founded by Leslie White and chaired by Roy Rappaport. The people in the department and I did not agree on many things. Their strong positivist bent was orthogonal to my interpretive, humanistic interests.

I stayed for two years, but my interests in anthropology were theoretical not regional. My original regional interests, such as they were, were in us, the anthropology of the United States. However, those in the department were fairly traditional and believed strongly in the value of the truly cross-cultural experience.

My interests were still strongly in language and culture and in literature. So I looked for a geographic region in which Michigan faculty had expertise and that had an indigenous literature or at least some consciousness of language. I immediately discarded China as a possibility, although there were some well-known "China watchers" such as Norma Diamond in the department at the time. (China was still closed to researchers then.) I couldn't learn the language well enough or quickly enough, and several thousand years of literary history was somewhat daunting. My theoretical hero was, of course, Clifford Geertz, who had done work in Indonesia. Indonesia had a conscious national language policy and was a multilingual country with interesting issues of diglossia, bilingualism, and other language and culture concerns to explore. As the national language was adopted only in 1928, its literature would be manageable. Besides, funding was available, and some faculty had expertise. Interestingly, the funding was through the Foreign Language and Area Studies (FLAS) program, a federal government program that supported studies in various parts of the world.[1] However, when I looked at the list of areas covered, FLAS painted a picture of areas of US national security concern at the time: Eastern Europe, Central America, and Southeast Asia. I did some research with past award winners to explore any implicit expectations of service they might have encountered postaward and was assured there were none. So in my first brush with national security, I chose that fork in the road and signed up for FLAS funding for Indonesia.

I decided that Michigan and I were not a good fit. I transferred to Cornell and discovered postmodernism. I swam in the sea of Derrida's presence of the absence but got a good grounding in Southeast Asian studies and politics from people like Ben Anderson, Jim Siegel, and Tom Kirsch.[2] Jim Boone was my major professor, and Carol Greenhouse was a member of my committee. Her interest in the United States reinforced my belief in the relevance of anthropology to the United States. I was beginning to see how I could answer some of my questions about my high school friends.

My dissertation kept me focused on language and culture as I began an exploration of teaching Indonesian (the national language) in schools as a deliberate mechanism to unite a multiethnic nation. Relevancy to my early questions about Japanese at home/English at school and Spanish at home/English at school was clear. However, as I got further into education in Indonesia, I discovered the relevance of a third language after the national language (Bahasa Indonesia) and the local language. That language was Arabic. Until the beginning of the twentieth century for some privileged Indonesians and until the mid-twentieth century for most, the only formal education available for most Indonesians was an Islamic education. So even as my topic evolved into an exploration of language and epistemology (What does it mean to "know" the Qur'an if you recite rather than read it in Arabic, and how does that relate to "knowing" in a classroom where you speak the local language and Indonesian?), I began to scratch the surface of one of the world's great religions. I never dreamed that road would lead someday to participation in conversations about elusive religious fundamentalist groups in the streets of Baghdad.

Bigger choices lay ahead. I received my PhD just at the time the tail end of the baby boomers had moved through college. Enrollments were dropping, and departments were cutting back. It was easier in the early 1980s to get a faculty job as an English professor than as an anthropology professor. And back in those days, academe was the only acknowledged career path for anthropologists. So, what to do? I moved to San Francisco for a variety of personal reasons. At this time, I needed to make the final revisions on my dissertation and had to get a job, as financial support from the university pretty much ended with the dissertation defense. I could type, so I answered an advertisement in the newspaper and got a job in a marketing and public relations firm that served clients in the Pacific Rim. Soon, however, the small firm migrated into public relations for the burgeoning computer and high-tech industry in nearby Silicon Valley.

This was 1982. To anchor this in Silicon Valley time, IBM had introduced the personal computer in 1981. My dissertation was written on an IBM electric typewriter—all four drafts of it. (There were cut and pasted pages on the walls, the ceiling . . .) I paid someone to type it on a Xerox minicomputer.

I still have the 5.5-inch floppy disks, although I doubt there is a machine outside a museum that can read them. Silicon Valley was full of startups, high energy, lots and lots of money, and computer jocks who could write great code but who had no idea how to talk to the consuming public who didn't know or care about bits and bytes. I became a cross-cultural translator, taking techie language and concepts and translating them into benefits consumers could relate to. My cultural linguistics served me well.

I also learned to apply anthropological concepts of organizational structure, dynamics, and culture to the corporate environment. One of my clients was a venture capital company whose success depended on its ability to select successful companies. I learned to elicit the various definitions of *success* and used my anthropological knowledge to match corporate structure and evaluate corporate values against those endogenous definitions.

Am I wandering down side roads? Where is the military in the mix? Nowhere yet. But all these choices had consequences. I no longer understood anthropology solely in an academic context. I could see its application and communicate its value in real-world settings to people who couldn't spell anthropology before I showed up. When I responded to the question about the field of my PhD, the response was either, "Oh, do you dig? And how does that help me?" or a slightly embarrassed giggle, indicating the respondent had no idea what anthropologists did. I had experience and skill in translating between technical and lay populations. I learned how to learn fast, and I learned what to learn to make that translation effective. I was becoming comfortable with technology. I was gaining an understanding of the impact of organization on different kinds of endeavors such as science/research, manufacturing, sales, and marketing. I was learning the culture of small business and entrepreneurship, and I had been introduced to Islam. I was watching organizational cultures grow and develop and sometimes self-destruct.

After a successful tenure in Silicon Valley, I was hired by a Connecticut-based software company as its director of marketing. When it went bankrupt because of excesses on the part of the senior executives, I moved to Albuquerque, again for personal reasons. Another choice at a fork in the road with unforeseen consequences. Albuquerque is an odd town in an odd state. We get more federal dollars per capita here in New Mexico than any other state except Alaska and the District of Columbia metro area. As such, New Mexico is a land of contrasts. There are just under two million people in the whole state, about half of whom are in the Albuquerque area. There are three Air Force bases in the state, one huge Army missile test range (White Sands), and two of the nation's three nuclear weapons laboratories (Sandia is in Albuquerque;

Los Alamos is in Los Alamos, just north of Santa Fe; and the third, Lawrence Livermore, is in California). The state is very poor, ranking forty-fourth in per capita income and about forty-seventh in high school graduation rates. That said, Los Alamos County has more PhDs per capita than any other county in the country, and the two national laboratories pay their combined sixteen thousand employees nationally competitive salaries. It is a minority majority state, with about 45 percent Hispanics and 10 percent Native Americans.

It was into this small world I plunged when I arrived in Albuquerque. With my former husband, I set up a marketing services firm and used community engagement as a business development tool. My hi-tech experience in Silicon Valley served us well. *Technology transfer* was just becoming a buzzword, and the weapons labs and the university were encouraging their scientists and engineers to take technologies outside the fence to commercialize them. New Mexico's senator Jeff Bingaman was a strong champion of the notion and worked hard to get federal legislation passed that relieved some of the intellectual property barriers that were inhibiting the flow of technologies from the public to the private sector. Working with his office on some of these issues was my first foray into national politics. The labs and, not much later, the University of New Mexico established formal tech transfer offices, developed policies, and worked to open doors to the community to encourage startups and contribute to the economic diversification of central New Mexico.

I was involved in the thick of the efforts from many directions. I had as clients several companies that were established by scientists or engineers from the labs who wanted to commercialize technologies. I was president of the New Mexico Entrepreneurs Association, an advocacy and professional group for these emerging firms. We endeavored (among other things) to identify structural impediments to economic development, such as the lack of a critical mass of intellectual property attorneys or venture capital firms in the state, and to propose mechanisms to address these problems. I worked on projects with the city of Albuquerque to identify and stimulate key economic clusters. I supported the labs as they took on as a project the development of a research park just adjacent to the laboratories' boundaries. And in an effort that ultimately took up almost all my time, I started a microeconomic development nonprofit organization called WESSTcorp to help women start their own businesses and ran it for three years as executive director. While I never thought this last endeavor would be directly relevant to working with the military, I am finding the lessons learned in the small Hispanic villages of northern New Mexico and in consultations with women from Albuquerque's poor south valley neighborhoods are invaluable in discussions of peace and stability operations in Iraq or Afghanistan, or in getting a glimpse into life in an urbanizing Pakistani environment.

So my life in Albuquerque that first five years or so (1986–1991) was a highly stimulating mix of interaction with PhD scientists and engineers, entrepreneurial activity, women struggling to create different lives for themselves, endless rubber-chicken fund-raising lunches, board meetings, travel through the spectacular New Mexican countryside, sleeping on dirt floors in adobe homes, talking to people at companies trying to raise millions in venture capital—indeed a land of contrasts. I learned a lot. I developed my skills in cross-cultural translation, trying to explain business structures, processes, and language to scientists and engineers and to women, populations that had never seen a balance sheet and didn't understand cash flow. Working with Sandia Labs and lab personnel started to give me insight into the fascinating world of science organizations and, more specifically, the public funding of science for a particular purpose, called mission-directed science. The general failure of technology transfer endeavors aroused my curiosity about the underlying causes.

The Society for Applied Anthropology's annual meeting was in Santa Fe in 1989. I participated in a panel on economic development with a paper on the cultural roots of the failure of technology transfer. That caught the attention of some folks at Sandia, and they asked if I would be interested in pursuing a staff position in a new policy-related endeavor focusing primarily on science policy and related macrostructural questions. I had been investing pretty heavily in WESSTcorp for the previous three years, and while it was the most rewarding thing I had done to date, it also was one of the most emotionally intensive. I was burned out and thought that a switch from microeconomic development to work at the macropolicy level would be interesting and stimulating. I agreed. That, as it turns out, was not just a fork in the road but a major interchange.

The move to Sandia was a challenge for me and for the labs, serving an instructional purpose for us as we tried to introduce social science into organizations that are profoundly unfamiliar with it. As it turned out, my hiring by Sandia required far more than just development of a job description. It required a change in organizational culture and processes.

My hiring was directly sponsored and promoted by one of the four line vice presidents, and I went through the process Sandia had for hiring PhD candidates for technical staff positions. At the time, all these candidates were from the physical or engineering sciences, and almost all of them were newly minted PhDs. I was ten years out of school by that time, and certainly not from the physical or engineering sciences. However, I dutifully submitted transcripts all the way back to my undergraduate years (they had a hard time with Santa Cruz, as grade point average was one of the implicit hiring criteria, and I didn't have one), gave a technical talk on what would now be termed the *social study of science*, and had candidate interviews with guys who weren't quite sure what to ask. I passed all the hurdles, and my hiring package went to personnel with all the necessary approvals.

And there we ran into a problem. Technical staff at Sandia have degrees in a scientific or engineering discipline. Anthropology doesn't count. They were willing to hire me as administrative staff, but the labs are very status conscious (at that time your personnel designation was listed after your name in the labs' phone book), and the corporate culture is dominated by the PhD technical staff. Furthermore, pay scales are better on that side of the house, and opportunities for professional advancement are far better. Besides, I had a PhD from a highly reputable university in a recognized discipline, and Sandia was hiring me to work alongside technical staff members doing similar work; actually, as it was policy related, I probably was better qualified for the work than the scientists and engineers. So, what to do?

I decided that rather than make an abstract argument about the legitimacy of anthropology (again, which even many of my supporters couldn't spell), I would take a different route. I discovered a procedure for converting an administrative staff member into a technical staff member. It was being used at the time primarily to legitimize the large cohort of computer scientists who originally had been brought on in support positions but now were beginning to contribute directly to mission work. I found out what it would take to be converted, which consisted primarily in the demonstration of an ability to do technical work. I determined what technical work really meant (in itself an interesting exercise in cultural linguistics, but which generally boiled down to rigor and transparency in the research method) and promised others and myself that I would start as administrative staff, then develop a sufficient portfolio of such work within a year to be converted to technical staff, or I would leave.

And so it happened. Not only was I converted to technical staff at the end of a year, but I was promoted to manager at the end of the second year—almost a record, I was told, from time of hire to promotion. I then spent the next three years building a social science–focused department that was externally funded in the same way and by the same customers as other Sandia departments were funded. I could have taken an easier route and logged many thousand fewer airplane miles to the labs' customers who are primarily in Washington, DC, but I had learned something from my hiring experience. I could not gain legitimacy from my credentials. (Interestingly, it turned out to be important that my PhD was from Cornell, which had an outstanding physics department, and Sandia recruited heavily there. So although I doubt a single Sandian could have told you Cornell even had an anthropology department, I benefited from reflected glory.) However, I could gain legitimacy from practice. So I built a department that looked as much like other Sandia departments as possible, given that the work we did was somewhat different. It certainly didn't hurt that after the fall of the Berlin Wall in 1989 the Department of Energy's mission expanded into softer areas such as economic competitiveness, and national security concerns expanded into areas such as worries about the human capital associated with the nuclear complex of the former Soviet Union. In fact, by the end of those five years, personnel in my department were getting requests from others across the labs to participate on their projects, and we were drawing other departments into ours.

I write this not to blow my own horn but to emphasize a lesson I learned the hard way. We can gain legitimacy in many ways. Certainly we all wish our credentials to stand on their own merit, and the depth of knowledge we gained through all those years at school to be directly applicable to our professional problems. After all, a great deal of blood, sweat, and tears (not to mention dollars) are tied up in that dissertation. However, to a world unfamiliar with anthropology, we are going to have to prove our worth through practice. This is particularly true in the military world, as the military is inherently an operational culture. We must learn to effectively translate our capabilities into a language and format relevant to military activity and develop skills that will allow us to communicate our offering to them. Then, particularly in the early years, it is critically important that we deliver the highest-quality work. This means work that conforms to ethical standards, exhibits rigor in method, and is performed with integrity, even if it results in an answer the sponsor does not expect or want. Yes, we do have to prove ourselves. If we are not useful, they will discard us.

Lest I sound too altruistic to be real, I now confess that I became highly frustrated by the bureaucracy of a large, quasi-government organization, and my apparent inability to develop a real appreciation for the social sciences in the labs. I was asked one too many times, "And tell me why we need an anthropologist? What exactly do you do that I couldn't do?" My inability to see that I was making any difference in the labs or in Washington took its toll. So in 1998, I quit. I took a brief excursion for a couple of years into the environmental arena, working primarily on public participation in governmental decision making and risk communication. I had started a small consulting business, so I maintained my relationship with the labs, working on a project basis with them. Most of my work with the labs from the late 1990s through the early 2000s was in the organizational and management arena, helping labs' leadership better understand and leverage their own organization (structure and culture) so they could be better stewards of the tax dollars they were allocated. For example, I investigated the safety culture at Sandia, conducting interviews and focus groups with staff and management across the labs, ranging from represented union workers to university-trained PhDs. I ensured that these types of data collection projects were designed and executed with methodological rigor and complied with all requirements of the Human Studies Review Board. The output of the work went through briefing high in the management chain and provided input to practice revisions focusing on ensuring that everyone went home with the same number of fingers and toes with which they started the day. This work was complemented by a similar study I was conducting at Intel Corporation's large fabrication plant in the Albuquerque area. The parallel studies highlighted some interesting differences between the organizational culture and resulting behavior at public and private sector organizations that informed both studies. I also participated in a project in which we (the labs and I) worked closely with the Mexican government to set up a joint technology-based economic development effort along the US-Mexican border, focusing and expanding the labs' technology transfer and outreach efforts. This drew heavily on my WESSTcorp experience and required understanding community, regional, and national goals, as well as the differences in work styles and public policy processes on both sides of the border. I supported the labs in their work with the intelligence community on a wide variety of projects. I did some work directly with the nuclear weapons people, looking at decision-making processes and the impact of laboratory organizational structure and culture on effectiveness in certain types of development efforts.

Was all this anthropology? You bet! The success of the analytic projects depended on rigorous method, combining knowledge gained by participant observation in the community with data collection through focus groups and interviews, supplemented by secondary source research. The analytic frames for project definition and in the execution of the analyses were drawn from my theoretical training in social and cultural anthropology. My products came complete with footnotes and bibliographies grounded in the theoretical literature, although most were not published as they were management proprietary.

Until this time, my work had been with the national security community, not directly with the military. I worked with intelligence organizations and with those involved in the design, production, and maintenance but not use of nuclear weapons. I was involved with a complex that engaged in research and development to support the national security enterprise and, as such, also did work for the military. But my contact with the military was one step removed, through the veil of the labs.

All this changed with September 11, 2001. I do not need to go into detail here about the military's frustration with fighting an enemy who never appeared on the battlefield, did not seem to have a formal doctrine, and came from a profoundly different cultural tradition. Washington agencies from the Department of Energy to the intelligence community and the newly created Department of Homeland Security began to turn to their research and support organizations with questions about motivation, intent, organizational structure, and the like. All of a sudden, social science, and anthropology in particular, became very popular. There was no overnight increase in understanding of the culture concept or in what we could bring to the table in terms of increased understanding, but organizations appeared to have a need for a "pet anthropologist" to trot out to show that they were effectively addressing concerns that had been identified as key. Pardon my cynicism, but after a decade of benign neglect if not outright dismissal, it was rather irksome to have the national security community discover that the adversary's culture matters. It always mattered. It mattered during the Cold War. We in the West now use *culture* as a descriptive not normative term, a relatively recent development (late nineteenth century). The normative baggage is still not completely absent, as we often still see equations linking culture and civilization in Western discourse. Interestingly, however, there are instances of current use in which the valences have flipped. Now it is "they" who have culture, not us. When I inform military colleagues that I am an anthropologist, they immediately assume that I have knowledge of "them." When I go on to say that I am interested in the culture of the United States, that our culture plays as important a role in the conflict as "theirs," there generally is a pause as they process that thought. The outcome is agreement, but it is interesting to find that the folk definition of *culture* in our national security community is now a catchall term to explain the inexplicable, to appropriate the odd. In this definition, our normalcy needs no such explanation.

Sandia had connections to many parts of the national security community including the military. As problems and issues changed from the Cold War, a technology-heavy portfolio to the more human-centered problem of the new security environment, many of the labs' projects and programs required social science expertise. So I met the military.

Through this path I participated in a series of workshops sponsored by the US Special Operations Command (USSOCOM) on behalf of Sandia.[3] The organization responsible for the management of the workshops was a new endeavor sponsored by USSOCOM called the Joint Special Operations University (JSOU), designed to educate special operators and military leaders in areas specific to joint special operations. JSOU conducts classes at its home campus (MacDill Air Force Base, Tampa, Florida), at military bases around the country, and overseas. Students are US military personnel, other members of the national security community, and from foreign military and law enforcement.[4] JSOU also supports research by students at the military colleges and by its senior and associate fellows on topics of particular interest to special operations, which it publishes through a monograph series. Courses range from two-week seminars in irregular warfare to two-day executive seminars on interagency activities in combating terrorism.

I was invited to become a senior fellow at JSOU. Anthropology was of particular interest to special operations forces (SOF) as they have a strong interest in indigenous populations and regional knowledge. Although there are females (the military term) in Civil Affairs and Psychological Operations (two organizations that historically have structurally been moved in and out of the special operations world), the iconic Special Forces A-teams and Navy SEALs teams are combat units, precluded by law from including females. I was the only female senior fellow. At many JSOU and USSOCOM meetings, I am the only woman participant, although other women are present as part of the support staff. In many cases, I am the only participant with no combat service or, indeed, any military service. When I teach for JSOU, there often are no women in the class.

The military personnel treat me with unfailing respect. I always have felt there was an appreciation for what I brought to the table and no criticism for my absence of experience in certain areas. While I am always challenged to make the anthropology relevant, I never presume to have military field experience and always speak from my own experience. Whenever possible, I try to solicit stories from my students and associates and use these stories as examples of anthropological principles in action. In fact, it is my acceptance that has led to difficulties. I was part of a JSOU team that went overseas to a Muslim country to conduct a class. I was the only woman in the JSOU contingent, and it took many requests for detailed information about dress codes before I got beyond the business attire response. Was a skirt okay? (It was.) Did I need to cover my head during the class or on walks through the city? (No.) I also have been on military bases in areas dedicated to combat units. No women.

No bathrooms for females. We worked it out. I often ran into similar problems regarding my civilian (rather than military) status when teaching on military bases in the United States. As a civilian with no prior military experience, and so no military ID, I found getting onto a military base is not a trivial matter. As almost all the other JSOU participants are prior military, they often forgot to do the administrative work that would allow me access. My complete acceptance into the community blinded them to my special requirements as a woman and a civilian with no military history.

My work at JSOU and with USSOCOM helped introduce me to the very foreign culture of the US military and the even more specialized culture of special operations. I learned about the distinctions among the services and the importance of rank. I learned about combatant commands or COCOMS and the crosswalk among COCOMS, the military services, and the civilian world of the Office of the Secretary of Defense. It may have helped that my initial entrée to the world of the uniformed military was through SOF, which has always worked through, with, and by indigenous populations, and so has an institutional and personal appreciation for the types of insight cultural knowledge can bring. They also tend to be better educated than those in the general purpose forces and often have had some contact with the concept of culture. They are older than people in the general purpose forces, because the Army Special Forces, which makes up the bulk of SOF, requires prior military experience. An anthropologist was not as foreign to them as she was to a nuclear weapons physicist.

So exactly what does an anthropologist do in these venues? I have long been interested in the ways organizational structure and the values it implies and engenders through its actions can implement and shape organizational policy and direction (shades of Clifford Geertz, and models of and models for). After 9/11, for example, the military discovered social networks. As anthropologists we know (a) social networks have been around as a social phenomenon since God made dirt; (b) theoretical analyses of social networks, while not that old, have been around for decades; and (c) no organization is a pure network. Early in my engagement with USSOCOM, I was participating in a military exercise to develop some of the planning documents for what was then called the Global War on Terror. Participants were discussing the development of a global counterterrorism network. In true military fashion, they began to discuss tasking the network and developing plans and schedules. As I listened to these new converts, it became clear to me that most did not really understand the relationship of organizational structure to organizational culture and effectiveness, nor did they know much about the operational benefits of other structures. So I published a monograph through JSOU on that topic (Turnley 2006), taught classes, gave talks, and often made a general nuisance of myself refuting the military mantra "It takes a network to fight a network." I also pursued an extensive case study of the application of these principles, exploring how the establishment of the USSOCOM as a formal organization in 1986–87, and USSOCOM's recent elevation to the supported or lead command in our current conflict, had an impact on the nature of the loose community of SOF USSOCOM was designed to serve. I did not see my purpose as passing judgment on the creation and maintenance of this institution, but rather to help make explicit the benefits and costs of certain types of organizational structures so these could be factored into decisions about our own military organization. Again this work was supported by JSOU and resulted in a published monograph (Turnley 2008).

My point of entrée was the heightened interest in the military in the adversary's organizational structure. This certainly is a topic well within the purview of anthropology. There was a felt need to understand that structure so we could leverage it for our purposes and to be able to reorganize ourselves as social networks to reduce some of the asymmetry of the fight. In all these venues, my goal is never to prescribe a structure but to help leadership and others have a better informed understanding of the structures and organizations they work in so they may make better use of them to fulfill goals they have identified. In almost every case, I get a respectful audience that may not agree with me but is willing to listen and intellectually engage with the content.

A second area of my work is tool development and application. The military is very familiar with tools to address physical targets and the analytic support to project potential and assess actual effects. This arena has moved strongly in the direction of technology-based solutions. Social science in general and anthropology in particular are subject matter domains with which most in the military are not too familiar. Social science–based tools and techniques are generally not technology based, the data are often qualitative, and effects of programs and projects are difficult to measure. Not surprisingly, the military has defaulted to a certain extent to tools its people know well. Computational social science, the development of computer-based models of social organizations, has received a great deal of attention in certain parts of the military and the DOD. However, because few social scientists are familiar with these tools, many of these models have been built with little or no input from them. These models are only useful if the social theory that informs their structure is sound, and the data on which they are built have integrity. I have been supported by the Defense Threat Reduction Agency (a DOD agency) to research and write a white paper exploring ways computational social models are qualitatively different from models of physical phenomena. At the same time, I contribute to the construction of the structure of some models to ensure they are grounded in published theories of human organization, interaction, and culture. I have explored if and how concepts such as legitimacy can be appropriately operationalized in a computational model. I've looked at questions of communication, ideology, and political commitment in these same contexts. I also have challenged the use of these models as predictive tools since they cannot be validated in the same ways physics models can. I've addressed issues on the interdisciplinary conversations required for a theoretically grounded computer-based model of a sociocultural system. I write papers, give talks, participate in workshops and seminars, and work directly on projects that build these models. Many of the topics with which I am concerned have applicability far outside the military and national security communities.

I also have worked with some of the military services to develop more qualitative tools for teaching culture concepts. A project with the Marine Corps Intelligence Activity to develop vignettes, for example, required interviews of Marines recently returned from the Middle East and drew upon my ever-expanding knowledge of military culture. The challenge here was to develop something that was culture general enough that it would serve the Marines no matter where they were deployed, yet specific enough to the current conflict to be relevant.

Finally, I have contributed in the general area of language and culture. Not only does my anthropological background help here, but the work I have done in marketing and public relations is directly relevant. Strategic communication, psychological operations, and increased involvement of military personnel with local populations have raised awareness of the importance of effective communication. I teach various military audiences in this area. Perhaps fortuitously, my experience with foreign languages and cultures was not in the Middle East but in Indonesia and the American Southwest. Hence, I am able to stay away from a regional studies approach and teach general principles. This, hopefully, provides transferable knowledge rather than area-specific techniques.

It was a long road from Venice High School to the Pentagon. There were many roads not taken along the way and many decisions made that had unforeseen consequences. However, I believe all the roads I took were paved with anthropology (to stretch a metaphor until it screams), and all the roads were necessary for me to end up here. I was introduced to Islam through my PhD fieldwork. I became comfortable with technology in Silicon Valley, and as companies rose and fell at warp speed there, I had a wonderful laboratory to watch and learn about organizational development. I participated in the entrepreneurial community in New Mexico, which led me to microeconomic development, a key component in many of our stabilization operations today. I went from small business to a large quasi-public corporation, which gave me an opportunity to see the intersection of corporate culture and public policy. Through work with the weapons labs, I was introduced to the national security community that provides the policy context for the military. Finally, I met the military and was able to draw all these threads together. In all cases, my perspective on my subject was an anthropological one, and my methodology was participant-observation, semistructured interviews, and other tools of the discipline. What does organizational structure tell us? How are organizational values played out through behavior? What behaviors are implicitly rewarded? What is going on with communication? Can I describe the power structures? Elicit the different mental models held by different players? Understand how the instantiation of those models in behavior gives us the interesting scenarios we see playing out in the military community today?

I see my professional responsibility not as a cheerleader and uncritical supporter for the work of the military and the national security community, but in my own small way as a contributor to the effective and efficient use of national resources. I have been in explicit advocacy roles, such as the executive director of WESSTcorp. That is not the role I play in my relationship to the military. I see my role as using my professional background and knowledge to critique (not criticize) approaches and methods in national security and help others be more sophisticated, knowledgeable, and aware participants in their own organizations. I am a guest in their house. I am a participant-observer, looking from the outside in. I am not, nor have I ever been, a member of the military. However, I hope that my outsider status, in the true tradition of anthropology, will help me see some things those in the military are unable to see about themselves. If I can communicate well, it is just possible I might make a difference.

I disagree with many of the policy goals of the government, as, by the way, do many of the soldiers, sailors, airmen, and Marines I come into contact with. The military, however, is not a policymaking organization. It is an operational organization. Under our Constitution, which establishes civilian control of the military, policy decisions are made by presidential appointees and operationalized by career civil servants and the military. That said, recognition of the "fog of war" and the uncertainties of real life give a fair amount of institutional leeway to military personnel, particularly of senior rank, to make interpretive decisions within the boundaries of the policy space.

I provide my input to the policy process and national political position as does any citizen, including uniformed personnel in their role as citizens. Given that most countries have a military and intelligence service, and that this country publicly funds a huge research and development enterprise, I believe if I can make those organizations more effective I will have made a positive difference.

I can think back to several choices I have made in the past forty years that led to my current involvement as an anthropologist with the military. In very few of these cases did I have an inkling that the road would take me here. When I look back on this journey, I do not see an expedition that set out to engage with the military or contribute to national security, but a journey to better understand ourselves. As an American living in the twenty-first century, where could I find more fruitful engagement on this journey than with one of our biggest and most powerful social institutions?

Notes

1. FLAS was one of several programs funded under Title VI of the National Defense Education Act of 1958, designed to develop expertise in languages and culture that would support our national security needs. In addition to supporting students (such as myself) with scholarships, the program established some now very well-known regional and area studies centers at universities around the country. The Fulbright-Hayes Act of 1961, which has funded the doctoral research of many anthropologists (including me), was seen as providing an international dimension to the National Defense Education Act. For more information on these bills, see www2.ed.gov/about/offices/list/ope/iegps/history.html.

2. Although I did not realize it at the time, Cornell's Southeast Asian Studies Center was a National Resource Center funded by the National Defense Education Act.

3. USSOCOM is a combatant command that oversees the special operations forces of all the military services: the Army Special Forces (Green Berets), the Navy SEALs, the Air Force Special Operations Command, and the relatively new Marine Corps Special Operations Command (see US Special Operations Command 2010). It has a two-part mission: "Provide fully capable Special Operations Forces to defend the United States and its interests" and to "synchronize [US] planning of global operations against terrorist networks" (see www.socom.mil/Pages/Mission.aspx).

4. One of USSOCOM's twelve "core activities" is foreign internal defense, which as USSOCOM defines it, is "providing training and other assistance to foreign governments and their militaries to enable the foreign government to provide for its country's national security" (see www.socom.mil/Pages/AboutUSSOCOM.aspx). This covers the training/education of foreign personnel. The provision of classes for US military and civilian personnel derives from USSOCOM's two-part mission: to provide "fully capable Special Operations Forces" (www.socom.mil/Pages/Mission.aspx) and to synchronize US planning of counterterrorist operations.

Pebbles in the Headwaters
Working Within Military Intelligence

Kerry Fosher

Kerry Fosher's chapter follows her road of researching, advising, consulting, and teaching, which was motivated by a deep desire to help solve problems from an anthropological perspective. Her chapter begins with a process of self-discovery, wherein Fosher finds professional and personal satisfaction in making cultural scholarship and critical analysis relevant to government and later military work. For Fosher, ethics becomes critical as she considers not only opportunities for a lifelong career in military anthropology but an imperative to aid those not educated in anthropology who were implementing national policy at home and abroad. As Fosher says, "Choosing to engage has consequences, but so does inaction."

I came to the intelligence community (IC) and to national security–related work itself by an indirect route, an experience shared by many who work in the security sector. I became interested in the sociocultural construction of security as a graduate student at Syracuse University. Under the guidance of my mentor, Robert Rubinstein, I crafted a dissertation project on how the United States transformed ideas about national security through the daily practices of those working with organizations newly involved in security. I chose to do this through the lens of a newly emerging area of practice called *domestic terrorism preparedness* or *homeland defense*, looking at what happened when new voices—police officers, firefighters, doctors, city administrators—became involved in figuring out what it meant for the nation-state to be secure. I arrived at my field site, Boston, in June 2001. The attacks on September 11th, 2001, affected my work topically and methodologically. Over the next several years, I conducted research among responders and planners. I became interested not only in studying problems but also helping solve them, many times by adding an anthropological perspective (see Fosher 2005, 2009, 2010).

From my field site, I joined a new organization, the New England Center for Emergency Preparedness, at Dartmouth Medical School in January 2004. I worked in an applied/research capacity, trying to help local, state, and national organizations build saner approaches to emergency preparedness and homeland security in the chaotic environment that followed the creation of the federal Department of Homeland Security. In this position, I continued my intensive contact and collaboration with practitioners. Increasingly, I found professional and personal satisfaction in bridging gaps between academia and various levels of government. I enjoyed bringing scholarship and critical analysis to bear, not only at the level of policy development but also during implementation, where people at many levels grapple with the constraints and creative opportunities policy presents. I also found that my anthropological background was useful in a somewhat different way, in helping people reshape their organizations to cope with new concepts and new roles. This interest in organizational reshaping has been a theme in all my work for the past several years.

In late 2006 I was asked to take a position as a visiting professor at Air University at Maxwell Air Force Base in Montgomery, Alabama. My primary responsibility there was to start up the Cross-Cultural Competence Project, an initiative I shared with several people, including Brian Selmeski, who developed the initial concept. The project was an attempt to build an understanding of general cross-cultural concepts through service members' professional military education, which takes place over the course of twenty or more years. There were two operating assumptions, hypotheses that cannot really be tested except over the course of decades. The first was that given the grim realities of how the US Agency for International Development and the State Department are funded and trained, and barring a revolutionary change in our foreign policy trends, US military and intelligence organizations will continue to be tasked with civil and humanitarian missions for which there is no comprehensive educational plan. The second assumption was that a regional or culture-specific approach to teaching culture was not a sustainable option for service members who are deployed to many different locations over the course of their careers, often with little or no time to learn about the next location. We were successful in having the Cross-Cultural Competence Project chosen as the Quality Enhancement Plan for Air University. This tied the goals of the project to the university's reaccreditation process.

I visited with people from many other culture-related programs in all branches of the service during the time I was with the US Air Force (USAF). Over the course of these visits and conversations with colleagues, I became convinced there was an opportunity to shape the way staff at the Department of Defense (DOD) and in the IC think about culture. I also began to feel I had an ethical obligation to work with the people in these organizations who were in the unenviable position of having to implement national policy whether or not they agreed with it. As described in more detail in the next section, the young service member and the people the service member encounters while deployed do not get to wait for us to determine if we will change foreign policy. Choosing to engage has consequences, but so does inaction.

While those of us engaged in these efforts all understood we would not be able to change things in exactly the ways we might like, we began to get a vision of how small changes now could have significant impacts over time. We also recognized that some of what we managed to do would suffer from the public health dilemma. In public health, if you work very hard, get decent funding, and luck is with you, nothing happens. No outbreaks of polio, no foodborne diseases, nothing. Nothing is a hard product to keep selling. Some of what people working in the security sector do is like that. If we manage to get somewhat better language into doctrine, training, or education, and that leads to better decisions, nobody will ever know how things might have been different. We will never be able to conclusively demonstrate what we accomplish. Given those concerns, as well as the ethical considerations described later, I thought long and hard about whether to commit to this line of work and which organization or organizations would be the right venue.

The decision to take a job with an intelligence organization was not an easy one. Because I was only on loan to USAF, I could have gone home to New Hampshire and continued my work at Dartmouth Medical School. I had opportunities at several military universities that would have been far closer to a traditional academic career and less ethically problematic. I could have done private contracting, picking and choosing the projects I liked and having a more flexible working environment. All of these would have been easier and more financially sound than the job I chose at Marine Corps Intelligence Activity (MCIA). In the end, the choice came down to two factors. I had worked with Marines and was impressed by the work they were already doing and their version of professionalism, which included being able to tolerate uncomfortable perspectives. (Like Paula Holmes-Eber, I also found the institutional culture of the Marine Corps fascinating.) I also was increasingly aware that the way the IC was addressing culture was something of a black box, not only to the civilian academic world but even to those of us working in military training and education communities.[1] Somebody needed to go learn about what was happening. After many discussions with colleagues, I decided that that somebody was me.

Let me be clear. I was a complete babe in the woods with regard to being a civil service employee, let alone working in an intelligence organization. There were many surprises, often unpleasant. Time cards? Inflexible schedules and work locations? Dress codes? Having to have what seemed like every little thing passed up through a chain of command for approval? Computer systems that seemed to be barely one step up from DOS? It was like stepping back into the 1950s. Neither I nor the people hiring me knew the right questions to ask each other. We simply stumbled over them.

Most of the people at MCIA sincerely tried to make compromises to approach what I needed in a working environment, negotiations that interestingly were always far easier and more satisfactory with Marines than with other civilian leaders. Despite these efforts, the organization was never quite able to approximate the work or the working conditions to which I thought I had agreed. It struggled to provide structures and time for independent research. It is still grappling with where social scientists should be placed in the organization to balance direct contact with the workforce with the freedom to work on broader issues, such as policy and program design. This is in part because of the usual structural constraints one would expect. However, it also results from the fact that MCIA, like many military organizations, is in a period of significant change. The current conflicts have resulted in growth and changing priorities. Simultaneously, how much of that change will stick and how much will vanish as deployment tempos decrease is uncertain. Like most organizations, MCIA contains people who embrace change and uncertainty as opportunities, those who respond by trying as hard as they can to keep things exactly as they are by any means necessary, and many who are somewhere in between. I've done my best to pass along lessons learned to others considering government service and to learn from my own mistakes.

MCIA—Context, Work, and Anthropology

Contextual Factors
Before spending too much time explaining what I do on a daily basis, it is worth highlighting a few things about military intelligence that may be a bit counterintuitive for some readers.[2] I do not work as the only civilian in a building full of Marines. Most military intelligence organizations in the United States

have both civilian and military personnel. The civilians sometimes outnumber the servicemen and servicewomen by a considerable margin. Some civilians even deploy; although in those situations, the balance between uniformed and civilian personnel is reversed. Civilian intelligence personnel can be either civil service employees or contractors.

In terms of structures and emic understandings, the most critical for the purposes of this chapter is the distinction between analyst and collector. In military intelligence, the people who analyze data and produce reports generally are not allowed to go gather these data in the field. They may conduct the equivalent of library research or go on overseas familiarization trips, but systematic research in the field is not allowed. They generate questions or requirements for the collectors. Collectors, specifically human intelligence collectors, are the people who go into the field. They are not supposed to do analysis or interpret what they see except in very limited ways. My work at MCIA was predominantly with analysts.

Also, not everything intelligence organizations do is classified or based on spying. Rather, a lot of emphasis is given to so-called "open source materials." For the moment, this tends to mean media, blogs and websites, and similar materials. (The IC as a whole has extremely limited access to scholarly resources. There is nothing equivalent to the kind of online journal access that every first-year undergraduate student has at most universities.) Generally speaking, a report becomes classified only because some part of the sources or methods used to generate the report is sensitive. If the report became available, people would be able to infer how the United States got the information, perhaps giving away secrets related to our technological capabilities or endangering a person who has given assistance. The use of the FOUO (For Official Use Only) designation is more complex. In some cases, it is used to ensure that an idea in development is not construed as a final government policy. However, as one might expect, it also seems to be used to cover dirty laundry, to enable a knee-jerk avoidance of Freedom of Information Act requests, and sometimes just out of habit. For these reasons, as well as normal anthropological protection of people who have helped me learn about intelligence, I end up having to write about my work in fairly generic ways.

MCIA produces information for Marine Corps commanders but also for other services and for the larger IC. In terms of basic culture-related products, it generates open source deep studies of countries, short field guides, and the now infamous smart cards that can be carried in a cargo pocket as a quick reference. Some of these are produced at MCIA. Others are contracted out to companies or think tanks. To varying degrees, based on background, interest, and tasking, MCIA's analysts also incorporate culture-related material into their regular briefings, reports, and other products. Often, these products are narratives, although PowerPoint briefings and visual aids such as maps are also common.

For the first two years I was there, I worked in a small "Culture Branch" before being moved to a different level that gave me broader scope across the command, but most of the personnel who were supposed to be addressing culture were employed in the regional branch structure. Most branches had responsibility for a particular region of the world (there were also branches with responsibility for geospatial and other types of products, but my interaction with them is limited). In the IC, regions are defined and redefined based on a calculus that continues to elude me, but the primary unit in this calculus is still a nation-state. MCIA is the smallest member of the IC. Consequently, most analysts were responsible for more than one country. A handful of analysts were tasked with looking at issues that transcend nation-state boundaries. Others incorporated a non-nation-state perspective, not because of tasking, but because they realized that humans have never really lined up neatly according to the structures we put on a map.

Each branch balanced its work between fulfilling requirements from the Marine Corps or other stakeholders and developing "initiative products" that allowed analysts to research and write about a topic they felt might be of importance in the future. The organization and, consequently, the tasks given to the analysts were driven by a tension between supporting deployed Marines and supporting the larger IC. While the former remained at the heart of the organizational identity, the latter was what paid the rent.

Work

MCIA leadership created the position of command social scientist and hired me with a variety of goals in mind; fortunately, it was a fairly open collective mind. I was to do some sort of training or education that would help the analysts bring more social science perspectives to their products. They hoped I would be able to improve the quality of their culture-related products and help them steer research funds in the right direction. MCIA wanted me to provide input on how the command developed programs and structures to address sociocultural issues in its work.

In reality, figuring out what needs to get done and balancing that against what is possible in the short term and long term given existing institutional orientations consumed most of my time. In terms of how I spent my days, the following categories are perhaps the easiest way of rendering und the deluge of possible activities and the way I think about them.

Teaching and mentoring. The work I did that is most readily understandable to most anthropologists was teaching and mentoring. In the way the Marine Corps is structured, a separate element, the Training and Education Command (TECOM), normally handles all training and education. (Contributor Paula Holmes-Eber works in two organizations within TECOM.) What I did at MCIA is, therefore, a little unorthodox from an emic perspective.

I developed a program for analysts that introduces them to sociocultural approaches and theories in small doses over the course of two years. Because all analysts had other educational opportunities, I balanced the program between perspectives I thought they could use immediately and things I thought would prime the pump by encouraging them to learn more through self-study or other outside classes. My focus was on displacing the state-centric and structural-functionalist approaches to culture that are common in the IC and instilling ideas from practice theory and processual approaches. After about a year, MCIA hired a second social scientist with a very impressive interdisciplinary background. He took over responsibility for some parts of the training and education work, and our theoretical and pedagogical discussions were some of the most stimulating and productive in my professional experience.

I also worked with other organizations that deal with training and education specifically for intelligence personnel, both analysts and collectors. These classes tended to be a few hours long with little or no time for advance reading, so I was mostly confined to getting across a few basic ideas about culture as process. To supplement these classes, I wrote a number of short pieces on basic social science concepts, such as reciprocity, identity and affiliation, and so forth. Most of these were intended to highlight a few concepts in the hope that the reader would seek more rather than give the reader a thorough introduction to the concept. However, we had surprising luck with this combination. Students read the materials and came back looking for more. Other instructors used the readings and course materials in different sorts of classes, helping the ideas become normalized.

Both kinds of teaching gave me opportunities to develop longer-term mentoring relationships. The mentoring cut both ways. I helped the students understand more about social science, while they helped me understand more about intelligence and the military. Ultimately, however, my focus on institutional shaping moved me away from direct contact with the analytic workforce, something that was a problem for me and the institution.

Product design and review. Initially, I often was asked to review products as they were released. My colleagues and I quickly came to an understanding that this was not the place where I could be most useful. When something came to me based on hopelessly flawed assumptions or insufficiently robust data, it was too late for me to make any productive contribution. As time went on, I was more likely to get involved in reviewing scopes of service for the products MCIA contracted out. What kinds of research would we require the contractors to do? What kinds of things would we expect to see in a bibliography? At what points would they be expected to explain the theories and methods they planned to use, and how much control would we have over those aspects? How would peer review be conducted? We also tried to work with the branches to ensure that if they contracted out a product, the contract addressed these sorts of issues.

I worked with parts of the command that were trying to create new kinds of products. We developed a small booklet that tried to give readers a sense of the sorts of cultural information they should try to understand when deployed. While there were (and still are) many checklists circulating, we tried with this booklet (with some success and some failures) to move beyond structural-functionalist checklists and get at the more processual aspects of culture. These sorts of culture-general products, as opposed to pieces more focused on imparting specific data about a group, grew in popularity among deployed servicemen and servicewomen. However, the data focus and regional structure of the IC mean there is still resistance to this type of product in stateside organizations.

Another major area of new effort at the time involved visualization. While many Marines are voracious readers, during operations the Marine Corps tends to prefer maps rather than narratives. So there is potentially great value in being able to map or otherwise visualize sociocultural considerations that might otherwise be left out of the planning discussion. As one might imagine, this is a particularly difficult problem. As an anthropologist, I tend to think that the most important parts of culture cannot be understood from a frozen diagram or reduced to lines and symbols on a map. However, working with the cultural geographers in MCIA helped me to see what could be accomplished within the limits of this sort of product.

Direct support to operations. While direct support for military operations has received the bulk of attention from the anthropological community and the press, it constituted a vanishingly small part of my work. I provided generic advice based on social science concepts for people with questions about how to work with local populations. Sometimes I wrote an e-mail with an anthropological perspective on an issue, such as the differences between rural and urban populations.

I made short trips to Iraq and Afghanistan to figure out what Marine Corps structures were in use or being created whose staff might be able to do more work on sociocultural issues. I never left military bases except to travel from one to the other. While I probably could have arranged interaction with the local population, there was no professional reason to do so, and I was not about to engage in the sort of war tourism that many straphangers insist upon as part of their travel experience.

Shaping. Much of my day was spent simply trying to shape discussions and questions so they were based on more realistic understandings of culture and what social science can and cannot do for the military. I think almost all social scientists engaged with the military spend a great deal of time in these efforts. At the risk of repeating myself, I will emphasize the fact that all these activities were undertaken with the assistance of the civilians and Marines with whom I worked. Many times they helped me think critically about my own ideas, and at the very least they helped me understand what I was trying to shape and to come up with the most effective ways to do so. The times when I ignored their advice usually ended in less than satisfactory results. Everything I did also was guided by the relationships I have developed in what we affectionately refer to as the *culture mafia*, the loose network of social scientists and others who were engaged in similar activities in other organizations. We tried to present a relatively unified voice on certain topics, helped each other think around corners, sort through ethical choices, and provided each other with the practical and moral support that was necessary to get through the day.[3]

I also worked with MCIA to develop more realistic programs for outreach to academia. For example, MCIA had a very good track record of interacting with outside academics for product review. However, it took some work to get some MCIA staff to understand that many social scientists become involved on the basis of personal trust relationships and only in certain capacities. So creating a big contact database that can be used by anyone is not likely to produce the result MCIA staff are seeking. In fact, it could undermine the relationships that various people in MCIA had already established.

On a broader level, I had many opportunities to contribute to discussions about culture at the level of the Marine Corps, the DOD, and the IC. These were not systematic, so I had to grab them as they came. A few examples may help illustrate the scope of these opportunities. Some arose as the result of MCIA's plans and strategies being circulated. This was the case with our education strategy, which got broad attention in the IC because of the efforts of my civilian and Marine counterparts. I had the chance to work with elements of the Marine Corps that were building the strategy for the service covering the present through 2025. In that instance, the chance was limited to showing how different approaches to culture can coexist peacefully so long as they are based on sound social science. I had many opportunities to provide input on what kinds of research got sponsored by various military and intelligence organizations. Much of this was limited to rejecting research agendas focused on technology in favor of sponsoring projects that help build understanding of sociocultural processes, especially in conflict or disaster situations.

There were fewer chances to directly influence the overarching policies that drive some of these smaller activities, but they did (and do) appear occasionally. I and several other contributors to this volume have been active in working groups responsible for developing policies that will guide how culture-related training and education will be conducted across the services. I worked with several groups in DOD and the IC that were struggling with the impulse to have standard definitions and taxonomies. While I doubt I did much to stop that trend in the short term, I was able at least to introduce a note of sanity by reminding people of simple things, like the fact that nobody in Afghanistan is going to feel compelled to abide by whatever definition of *tribe* eventually makes its way into official documents.

What is less easy to convey is how my commitment to shaping institutions, as opposed to simply implementing a training or research program, has shaped my life. The endless possibilities for shaping practices, structures, ideas, and so on, coupled with the knowledge that the window of opportunity was limited, meant that every day was a constant triage session. I scrutinized every activity in terms of balancing the things MCIA needed with other opportunities to create or support positive developments in the broader IC, the Marine Corps, or the DOD. I examined every decision for its potential impact on the uneasy relationship between social science and the military. Could this proposed program lead to something that will compromise the ethics of a social scientist, or is it structured in a way that provides appropriate firewalls and handholds? Could participation in this conference help keep me connected to important ideas and critiques from other anthropologists, or will it just be grandstanding? Is it more important that I attend a meeting about future directions for DOD culture research or that I write an internal memo on the appropriate uses of social scientists during deployments? Even absurd degrees of multitasking (one colleague and I had our strategy sessions by phone while cleaning our bathrooms) could only take you so far through the ocean of possibilities. I and anthropologists in similar positions continue to make hundreds of small decisions every day about where to place our attention. There are very few good choices. Except for rejecting projects that would compromise professional ethics, every decision to eliminate something by triage, to ignore an opportunity, is wrong.

Is It Anthropology?

All the preceding begs the question of whether what I did at MCIA was still anthropology. I think some of it fell pretty squarely into the realm of normal anthropological activities, such as teaching or research or mentoring. Other activities were straightforward applied organizational anthropology, trying to understand an organization and its people well enough to help them incorporate new ideas and activities. However, some of my daily work clearly blurred or crossed a line between anthropology and being an adviser whose work is informed by anthropology.

It strikes me that this is fairly common for anthropologists who work in advocacy or applied settings as opposed to working in predominantly academic contexts and occasionally taking on an applied or advocacy project. However, I think this aspect of the work has largely gone unmarked in the anthropological discourse, as we focus on activities we see as being within our purview. The lingering questions of what it means to do anthropology and what it means to be an anthropologist remain. What activities are in and out of the discipline? What combinations of activities and credentials make one an anthropologist? To what degree does self-identification play a role? While work in military or intelligence contexts highlights these questions because of contemporary debates, they have existed before and will not be solved if they are considered only in light of this particular context of practice.

Engaged With Whom?

From time to time, we all fall into the trap of talking about working with institutions or organizations (or even more ephemeral things, such as the national security state). Of course, the reality of engagement is much more human, more personal. I often talk about the fact that all my efforts to integrate social science are done *with* people not *at* them. I have partners where I work, Marines and civilians. For me to integrate social science concepts, I have to understand the programs, job tasks, current education, institutional context, and the constraints of my audiences—in short, the organizational cultures in which I will be working. I need to understand how people in these organizations are already thinking about culture. What are the opportunities and obstacles these existing frameworks represent? I also need help understanding the simple logistics of how to get things done in a very large and sluggish bureaucracy. Mary Douglas's (1986) work on institutions is some help in this regard, but nothing replaces a native informant. We each have some piece of the puzzle.

Another common pitfall in talking about engagement crops up in conference talks and question-and-answer sessions. We have a tendency to discursively place the people of military and intelligence organizations into polarized categories. We talk about mysterious all-powerful senior leaders whom we represent as having nearly limitless ability to secretly shape government activities for political and corporate ends. On the other end of the spectrum, we talk about young servicemen and servicewomen who join out of some misguided sense of patriotism or a desire for a better career and college funds, not realizing they will become pawns in a corrupt system. People are represented as either powerful, corrupt, and unaccountable, or as dupes. Of course, some people fall into these categories, but the vast majority of the people I encounter are neither omnipotent nor powerless. The reality is as complex and changeable as it would be in any other group in any society.

The occupational categories and power positions of the people I worked with at MCIA included active duty military personnel (mostly Marine officers and enlisted personnel), federal civilian employees, and contractors. I worked with people in significantly different power positions in the government—a brand new corporal, a civilian analyst fresh out of college, a senior analyst with twenty years of experience in different intelligence organizations, a retired enlisted Marine who returned to the organization as an administrator, a colonel, a general officer, and a member of the senior executive service, the civilian equivalent of general officers. The combination of military background, IC background, educational background and level, specific past experience, current job position, connections, and personality entered into a sort of calculus of how much of what kinds of influence a person had. One also had to consider whether the person was attempting to influence things through formal or informal channels. This calculus is not much different from what you would see in a university or other civilian organization.

It's a bit harder to pin down other aspects of people's personal identities. While the Marine Corps has created a very strong identity factor, which almost all Marines seem to absorb and foreground, many of the common stereotypes simply do not apply. In my current position, and at MCIA, I work with conservatives and liberals and people who don't fit in either category. I work with people who are simultaneously strongly patriotic and extremely critical of the government policies they enact. Some people seem to be working in intelligence for a regular paycheck and retirement benefits. Others have turned away from far more lucrative careers because of a personal commitment to service of one sort or another. Some are anti-intellectual and consider anything that makes them uncomfortable to be fluffy intellectual crap. On the other hand, a sizable percentage of the Marines are far better read than I can ever hope to be and have open and curious minds.

These combinations yield patterns in terms of what people find most important. As with any patterns, these are not necessarily predictive of the behavior of any one individual. However, people who left military service within the past several years are more likely to be focused on the immediate military utility of any program or activity or product. Those who have spent most of their time as civilian analysts tend to be more interested in the craft and profession of analysis. There are other patterns. All of these bear on the kinds and degree of opportunity and compromise in any specific project related to integrating social science.

Ethical Challenges

It is worth pointing out that ethical challenges are not the only ones we face in our work. There are fascinating theoretical and methodological issues to be worked out. There are opportunities and difficulties that occur in working in a heavily interdisciplinary environment. There are the challenges of bridging gaps, or deciding not to, in our own discipline. There are many issues related to bridging levels of practice, for example, what can be implemented at the level of one command can be hard to sell at the level of policy. While these concerns are beyond the scope of this chapter, it is worth signaling that other things going on in anthropological work with the military are worth examination in the future.

This section is somewhat shorter than might be expected, but that should not be taken as an indication that I don't find the debates to be critical. Because of current disciplinary concerns, I have published several pieces about how I understand and navigate ethical challenges (e.g., Fosher and Nuti 2007; Fosher 2010). I have spent a good deal of time over the course of the last several years grappling with the ethical challenges inherent in any applied work, concerns specific to working for the US government, concerns specific to working with a military organization, and those that arise in the context of intelligence work. The degree of reflection required in my daily work has been substantial. However, from 2006 through January 2010, I also was a member of the American Anthropological Association's (AAA) Commission on the Engagement of Anthropology with the US Security and Intelligence Communities, charged with looking into engagement with the military and the IC. This provided me with at least weekly discussions about ethics with a range of people, some who found any engagement with the military to be deeply problematic. As is the case with many of my fellow commission members, I have found myself, not always willingly, publishing and presenting nearly exclusively on the discipline's ethical debates for the last several years.

For me, the concerns expressed by anthropological colleagues tend to fall along predictable lines, for example, concerns about enabling flawed systems, the potential to do harm to one's research community (whether directly or indirectly), different kinds of secrecy, and how one keeps a grip on a very slippery slope. Since each of these is addressed in my earlier publications (Fosher and Nuti 2007; Fosher 2010), I will just recap my own daily decision-making process.

Daily decision making. If you are working in a military organization, and you don't see the potential for missteps in following the AAA's *Code of Ethics* (2009), you either have a very unusual job or you aren't paying attention. Even the need to maintain a scholarly identity that has greater freedom than your institutional role requires careful planning and negotiation, as shown in the disclaimer in note 1. The current code of ethics is not very helpful in navigating a career outside the academy. It is up to each anthropologist to be constantly mindful in ways that can be exhausting. My process is convoluted but always includes the following aspects:

1. Preserve the ability to leave. This means some difficult choices about lifestyle and finances. It has meant struggling to maintain other job options in the face of a workweek that is usually in excess of sixty hours. It has meant some difficult conversations with colleagues about why I have not bought a house near Quantico, despite the low prices and other incentives. Instead, for the first three years I spent working with Marines, I lived in Q-Town, a tiny independent town completely encircled by the Marine Corps base. As Paula Holmes-Eber mentions in chapter 3, this was not the most beautiful setting. As I wrote this section, I heard the thudding of helicopters, a freight train, and a large cargo plane coming in for a landing. Although my commute was great (I was only a mile from my office), the tap water was mildly carcinogenic, the space was cramped, and I

was never truly away from work. It was a far cry from my home in New Hampshire. However, it was inexpensive and did not tempt me to put down roots. For somebody with family responsibilities, this kind of tenuous relationship to life outside work would be very difficult to manage. Although I have moved away from Q-Town now, I still rent, still maintaining my ability to leave.

2. Maintain an intellectual bucket brigade. I work hard to maintain a network of colleagues up and down the spectrum of engagement. I like to think the circulation of ideas up and down the spectrum benefits everyone in it. However, there is little question that I am the one who is most in need of the connections. These colleagues help me recognize when I am sliding a bit farther down the slippery slope. They help me think through the ethical considerations in new projects. They keep me connected to theoretical and methodological developments in the discipline. Sometimes these conversations are more than a little uncomfortable, but they are necessary to ensure that the choices I make are conscious ones, not accidental slides driven by my gradual absorption of contextual biases. I use the differences among my colleagues to help make my decisions strong.

3. Be systematically vigilant. On daily, weekly, and monthly time lines, I revisit aspects of my work and the Code of Ethics, sometimes with members of the bucket brigade. One ethical justification of the decision to become involved with the military followed by passivity is not sufficient. Most of us working in these contexts are in situations where our work, as well as its context, changes frequently. You have to pay attention and do it rigorously. This may seem overdone to some, but I see it as a necessary preventive measure.

Obviously, this system is less than ideal. The AAA is revising the *Code of Ethics*. I am hopeful the revision will include better guidelines for those working outside the academy. I am aware that the revisions might also include provisions that place the sorts of work I do outside the bounds of what AAA considers to be acceptable practice. I feel comfortable that through my work on the commission and in other venues, I have had my say and am willing to live with whatever is the outcome of the revision. The important thing is that the discipline makes a conscious and informed decision.

Why?

I am often asked if, setting aside the ethical debates, there are any positive reasons other anthropologists should care about what I do or pay any attention to what I have to say about it. I tend to focus on four interlocked reasons, beyond those articulated in my earlier writing on ethics.

First, I don't agree that the issues of ethics should be construed as a source of negative attention. The pull from government to get anthropologists involved will wax and wane. With every resurgence of government interest in the discipline, an opportunity to reexamine existing and possible relationships surfaces. Anthropologists who have chosen to work in government are reminded of the concerns of their discipline. They may become reengaged, bringing new ideas and critique back to their organizations. Anthropologists who know little beyond headlines about government as an arena of daily human practice may come to have a more empirical understanding of the human side of the institutions they critique. Most urgently, we are opening this discussion at a time when our opportunity to learn from the past is still robust. In another decade, that may not be the case. Many anthropologists who were involved in these debates during the Vietnam era are in or nearing retirement. Those who were involved during World War II are even scarcer. If the relationship between the discipline and government is to be reconsidered, we should do so at a time when these voices are still available to us.

Second, as mentioned earlier, the issues highlighted by work with the military or intelligence organizations are not confined to those contexts. Many, such as the potential for sponsor-based bias, transparency of research design and results, and whether what we do is actually anthropology are equally relevant for other kinds of applied work and advocacy. The current debates are an opportunity to dust off some old questions about the position of applied work in the discipline and perhaps craft some new ones about the position of advocacy.

Third, the collegial bucket brigade previously mentioned works in both directions. By maintaining my connections with colleagues who have different opinions, I help ensure that I bring the best concepts, methods, and critique to bear on the problems I address. I may not always be successful, but sometimes those ideas become part of the institution. In the other direction, I have the opportunity to bring data out of places that are often black holes or blind spots for anthropologists. Anthropologists study the military and other security institutions, and some have done participant observation. However, few have the kind of access and depth of experience that working within those organizations can bring. While some of us working with DOD and the IC may not be able to publish easily, we can help guide those who do. US military and intelligence organizations have a large footprint in the world. It is hard to understand or critique that footprint without understanding the lives and day-to-day practices that make up these institutions.

Fourth, many aspects of the work of military anthropologists (for lack of a better term) have the quality of public anthropology. We try to promote policy based on sound social science. We advocate ethical research practices and hold our organizations accountable. We bring these perspectives into places that would otherwise rarely hear them, let alone incorporate them. Perhaps most importantly, we often bring anthropology to people who would never have the opportunity to take a traditional course. As a discipline, we do not make anthropology particularly available to those who cannot afford a college education or who have to focus that education on something more likely to get them a job with only an undergraduate degree. Any time an anthropologist teaches military personnel, there is a good chance the instructor will be bridging a socioeconomic gap the discipline has done very little to close. All anthropologists have gone through the experience of having the concepts and methods of the discipline change the way they see the world, ask questions, and conceive of solutions to problems. Sometimes this change is significant, sometimes it is just another step in a direction the person was already headed. The same possibility exists in every class or meeting room whether that room is in a university, a government building, or a transport plane en route to Afghanistan.

None of these reasons contains a promise of revolutionary change. I have a healthy respect for the staying power of large institutions. The shared senses of meanings created by the people in military and intelligence organizations do shape and constrain the way people think, as is the case with any group. In the case of military organizations, the pressure to conform is very strong. However, the pressure to bring your fellows home alive is equally strong. In every military service there are people who are naturally intellectually curious. There also are people who are constantly looking for ways to improve their work, which they may construe in terms of kinetic operations but also see in terms of the ability to come up with alternative courses of action and to interact with local populations so everyone goes home alive. This sounds overly simple in a chapter on anthropological practice, but it is quite real to the people with whom we interact. It creates an opportunity for small changes that can accumulate over time. This particular form of public anthropology has the quality of pebbles in the headwaters of a very large river. Small changes can lead to significant differences downstream.

Author's Note

The views expressed in this work are the author's alone and do not represent the position of the US Marine Corps or any government organization. Relevant sections of this chapter were subjected to security review by the Marine Corps Intelligence Activity. No material was changed or removed.

Notes

1. Although Rob Johnston's (2005) ethnographic study of practice among intelligence analysts was a valuable resource, the book was not designed to describe IC culture programs and predated many of the activities with which I was concerned.

2. As I was completing this chapter, I accepted a new position in the training and education realm of the US Marine Corps. I made this decision in part because of the issues described in the previous section and because of my increasing understanding of the institutional context and the elements that are most involved in slow long-term change. In this chapter I preserve the present tense for information that is enduring and the past for information that may have changed since my departure from MCIA.

3. While this network still exists, it has become attenuated by increasing numbers of voices and the diversity of projects and institutional contexts in which we are engaged.

6

Ethnicity and Shifting Identity

The Importance of Cultural Specialists in US Military Operations

Christopher Varhola

Christopher Varhola, a military officer who is also an anthropologist, highlights the importance and potential for anthropologists to provide critical local perspectives to strategic-level organizations. Drawing from his own field experience as a soldier in Iraq, an ethnographer in Tanzania, and an observer in Sudan, Varhola identifies multiple forms of military operations that suffer from the absence of such academic expertise. His narrative makes clear that too often those who pay dearest for this deficiency are the traditional subjects of anthropological study. This chapter is unique in that its arguments are nested in linkages between analysis of specific cultural patterns and military operations. He recognizes the ethical dilemmas of engaging with the US military, while calling for greater collaboration. Finally, Varhola modestly describes the significant contribution he has made at institutionalizing processes to foster more mutually beneficial and acceptable military-anthropological partnerships.

In 2002 the government of Sudan (GOS) and the Sudan People's Liberation Army (SPLA) concluded a cease-fire agreement for the Nuba Mountains in Sudan. To monitor the delicate situation, an international agency, the Joint Military Commission (JMC), was established. JMC members faced the challenge of integrating into the society of South Kordofan to resolve issues that could lead to the resumption of violence. Such issues were invariably civil-military in nature and included conflicts over grazing areas, retribution killings, and banditry. The JMC, neither an exclusively military or civilian organization, was initially led by a Norwegian general and included active, reserve, and former military members from eleven countries. It also contained foreign ministry officials from France and Canada, US State department contractors, civilian scholars, a medical doctor, and human rights workers. This mix of people allowed the JMC to better understand the operating environment and adapt to the changing conditions in the Sudan. I was one of two anthropologists who were part of this contribution, and the lessons we learned reinforced my belief for scholarly inclusion in military activities.

In a world of over seven billion people, there are no exclusively military operations. The world is composed of humanized landscapes in which all militarily significant terrain has some sort of human presence. As such, all conflict and military activities have civil, and thus cultural, dimensions. Within this framework, elements of culture and ethnicity are intertwined in a mutually transforming relationship with the causes and activities of armed conflict. Adding to this, the flexible attributes of ethnicity can be used to further the interests of warring or controlling parties. The US military is increasingly forced to confront such complexities but is often without tools for adequate understanding.

Understanding complex social processes is fundamental to lessening the negative impacts of military operations on civilians. In such settings, scholars can play an important role. US involvement in Iraq, however, presents ethical challenges for scholars, and many have declined public association with the Department of Defense. In addition to failing to enhance US military understanding of social dynamics in Iraq, this has also discouraged much-needed and less controversial scholarly-military collaboration in civil-military activities in other parts of the world. Such activities may include humanitarian demining, peacekeeping, disaster assistance, countering genocide, combating HIV/AIDS, and engineering and medical activities directed toward civil populations.

My intent in this chapter is to sidestep the polarized debate on Iraq and Afghanistan and draw attention to the importance of social scientists, particularly anthropologists, in collaborating with the US military in activities other than direct combat. I examine some of the ethnic and cultural complexities I have faced in military activities in the Middle East, Sudan, and East Africa. I also provide an overview of the newly established Social Science Research Center (SSRC) in the US Africa Command (AFRICOM) that is designed to provide US military planners with a formal mechanism to access abundant scholarly knowledge and advice.

As an armored cavalry officer in 1991 serving as a tank platoon leader along the Euphrates River in the middle of the Shiite uprising in Iraq, I experienced firsthand the need for cultural awareness and regional understanding in military ranks. Like the rest of my unit, I did not speak Arabic, nor did I possess a basic sociocultural understanding of that part of the world. Later I began to comprehend my small role in the ongoing tragedy of US involvement in Iraq. These events prompted me to learn Arabic and transfer to the US Army Civil Affairs and Foreign Area Officer Programs. They also piqued my interest in anthropology. My decision to leave the active military and become an anthropologist came in the aftermath of US involvement in Somalia. Although I never deployed to Somalia, I was disheartened at how the best of intentions resulted in further social collapse in a geographical area best now described as a failed state. The inability of US military forces to comprehend the social and economic dynamics of Somalia contributed greatly to the deterioration of the situation and the increased reliance on violence as a means of communication.

Given its unique skill sets and capabilities, the US military can contribute to an array of civil-military activities. In spite of this, it has traditionally placed little priority on regional expertise, except among its small group of foreign area officers, and to some extent, its special operations and civil affairs personnel. The study and integration of culture has generally been compartmentalized into a single staff section, meaning that the civil affairs or intelligence staff officer would give a briefing on local culture. Far from integrating cultural analysis into all aspects of military operations, this reduces cultural understanding and ethnic dynamics into what Robert Rubinstein (2008, 12) refers to as "traveler's advice." Peacekeeping, for example, requires superb situational awareness to allow forces to operate in ambiguous situations without becoming participants in the hostilities. It is folly to think that cease-fire and peacekeeping operations can be effective without close collaboration between multiple actors, which include soldiers, diplomats, academics, and public health specialists. This is all the more challenging in the midst of armed conflict, where sides become polarized, moral economies are undermined, and senses of limits are skewed. Identity shifts are further accelerated in conflict settings through the disruption of delicate trade relations and collapsed social services. Subsequently, individuals are often forced to clarify group affiliation. As a result, reliance on preconflict models of culture and society may be misleading. However, current research that is operationally integrated can make the difference between success and failure.

The AFRICOM SSRC, established in January 2010, is one effort to address these challenges in the JMC. As SSRC's first director, I was responsible for creating operating procedures, implementing ethical guidelines, and nesting the center with military planning and decision cycles. The initial structure comprised twelve scholars chosen on the basis of experience in Africa and a record of publication and research. It included economists, anthropologists, political scientists, and historians. I was the only member of the center who was a government employee. All others were hired under long-term contracts. In addition to our own research, the SSRC acts as a mechanism to cultivate relations with scholarly communities. To this end, we participate in and hold conferences. We also hire scholars on a short-term basis to conduct research of shared interest as a means to accommodate summer breaks and sabbaticals.

Based on the most salient challenges facing Africa, the SSRC does not focus on countering terrorism or violent religious extremism. Rather, it endeavors to understand dynamic social processes, attitudes, and ecological factors. To most Africans, crime, soil erosion, and clean water carry more relevance than international terrorism. Our methods are primarily ethnographic and focus on smaller geographically defined units of analysis. This approach highlights a critical difference between scholarly methods and those that might be more focused on "actionable intelligence." In addition to applied research, we attempt to make theoretical contributions, especially in the fields of conflict resolution and natural resource management. To this end, the SSRC has been successful in developing close ties with governmental agencies, peacekeeping institutes, and academic organizations in Africa. Peacekeeping training centers in Africa, for instance, train peacekeepers, election monitors, and land mine removers (deminers) for deployment into conflict and postconflict situations. The training therefore needs to be current and relevant.

Examples of SSRC research to date include an examination of sexual- and gender-based violence with excombatants in the Democratic Republic of the Congo, socioeconomic analysis in preparation of US veterinary and medical projects in Kenya, the training of US soldiers participating in a joint exercise in Mozambique, and the social and political dimensions of ethnicity in South Sudan. Such activities perhaps defy stereotypes of militarily relevant research, but they correspond to the noncombat orientation of AFRICOM. The sexual- and gender-based research is one element of attempting to create a responsible standing army in the Congo. Without nuanced understandings of the different types and contexts of sexual violence in the Congo, efforts by either the State Department or the Department of Defense would be viewed by the Congolese as superficial.

Peacekeeping: The Nuba Mountains of Central Sudan

Civilian populations are participants in conflict, both willingly and unwillingly. Some populations provide safe havens and logistical support for guerrilla forces and, as such, are often the targets of heavy-handed counterinsurgency operations. Other populations are caught between multiple armed groups and are victims of collapsed social services. Dedicated efforts to understand and protect the needs of civilian populations are critical. Effective peacekeeping often necessitates addressing poor infrastructure, usually in conjunction with UN agencies and nongovernmental organizations (NGOs). This presents risks, though, since humanitarian aid is subject to manipulation by warring factions, and no aid in a conflict setting can be entirely neutral. Consequently, perceptions of the United Nations were generally not positive in the Nuba Mountains during the time I was there. The various UN programs were often viewed as inefficient or biased toward one side or another. Some NGOs in the Nuba Mountains also became closely affiliated with either the Sudanese government forces or the SPLA. This state of affairs was frequently exacerbated by local leaders who claimed to be, and were externally recognized as, representatives of broadly defined groups.

It is a problem to categorize and construct group identities and motivations based on preconceived notions and stereotypes, especially in conflict where identities are subject to change and manipulation by the parties involved. Despite this, in the absence of nuanced regional understanding, military decision makers often have little choice but to create taxonomies of groups and ascribe interests and attitudes to these categorizations. In spite of its complexities, Sudan is still characterized by many leaders in the US military as a primarily religious conflict between the Arab Muslim north and the Christian and animist South. Not only does this give misleading categorizations of identities (as well as perpetuating a misunderstanding of animism), it also ignores the geographical gray areas of what indeed are the north and the south. Because of Sudan's size and heterogeneity, it is all but impossible to accurately characterize a broad Sudanese culture. This contest to narrowly define *national identity* fueled much of the fighting and has repeatedly stymied hopes of durable and lasting peace. The performance of Islam is heterogeneous, and there are wide ranges of religio-cultural orthodoxies and orthopraxies among the varied Muslim populations throughout Sudan. In recognition of this, in the Nuba Mountains, a locally produced 1991 fatwa specifically targeted Muslims who were not aligned with the GOS. The deviance from a state-sanctioned religion made them a threat to government efforts to religiously polarize the conflict.

Using ethnicity as a unit of analysis provides a tool for identifying and understanding the different social, economic, and political factors that influence identity shifts. It is worth repeating Joel Samoff's (1982, 19) ubiquitous maxim that "all people have multiple identities: which identity is salient depends on the situation." Religion, mode of livelihood, racial appearance, and language can each define group membership in a manner that is inclusive and exclusive. In Sudan, for instance, the imposition of Shari a law in 1983 attempted to fuse religion and the national legal code. In this framework, conversion from Islam could be simultaneously defined as a sin, a crime, and a political-military statement. Similarly, conversion to Islam in many cases was less a religious expression and more a survival mechanism. Ethnicity thus can be described as changing sets of related attributes that result in multiple overlapping identities. Of key value here is effective understanding of the conditions that accelerate change, as well as the analysis of factors and conditions that foment the overlapping, contextual, and fluid elements of ethnicity. Further, putting too much weight on one element of ethnicity can distort the larger social reality, as was arguably the case with many in the US military, who in the aftermath of the invasion of Iraq, categorized Iraqi society largely on the basis of tribalism and religious sectarianism.

Conflict analysis in the Nuba Mountains needed to accommodate a host of elements, which included contests for intrareligious control, conflicting modes of livelihood, competing geographical claims over declining arable areas, and maintenance of traditional ways of life. In this sense, cultural elements such as religion and ethnotribal identity signify affiliation with armed groups that control geographical areas. The choice of identity can be a life or death decision. As an example, throughout the 1990s one ethnotribal group in the Shatt area of the Nuba Mountains was composed of non-Muslim matrilineal agriculturalists. This placed them in a precarious position since their area eventually came under government control after intense fighting between GOS and the SPLA. Africans were often the targets of violence that included the arrest and forced conscription of military-age males and the military-economic raiding of people and food stocks by Muslim Baggara groups allied with the Khartoum government. As an element of an adaptive survival strategy, some villages collectively took active measures to transform their ethnic identity into that of the Baggara people to lessen their vulnerability in government-controlled areas (for a superb analysis of adaptive strategies in the Nuba Mountains, see Manger 1994).

Identity shifts can involve the transformation of ideals, practices, genealogy, mode of livelihood, and religion. Pastoralism and Islam are central elements of Baggara identity, and cow ownership distinguishes groups from traditional non-Muslim agriculturalists. Identity transformations have involved adopting fictive lineages that can be traced to the Arabian Peninsula, as well as symbolic transformations of modes of livelihood in which the ownership of cows became the new cultural ideal, although not a widespread reality because of widespread poverty. In such impoverished conditions, the possession of cows may actually be economically irrational. However, in the Shatt Daman area of the Nuba Mountains where I worked, the symbolic acceptance and physical possession of a limited number of cows became an ethnically distinguishable feature of recent converts to Islam.

Cows in much of Africa have cultural significance that goes beyond a purely economic value. Whereas this can be obvious and benign in a peaceful country such as Swaziland, in much of Sudan pastoralist lifestyles take on political-military dimensions. The association of pastoralism with Sudanese government forces, for instance, has transformed rituals and festivals concerning cows into idioms for government and Islamic domination of smallholder agriculturalists. At the beginning of the monitoring mission in the Nuba Mountains, our organization was duped into attending one such festival. Sudanese radio and television stations captured our presence and attempted to use this to show we were more supportive of the government than of the SPLA.

Much of this was learned only after the JMC monitors arrived in Sudan. The cease-fire in the Nuba Mountains initially had a limited intent to allow planting crops and delivering humanitarian aid. It soon became obvious that the military's knowledge of planting cycles and cattle migration routes were more important to fostering peace than understanding the military organizational structures of each side. As a result, the intelligence and security section of our mission was restructured to replace the traditional intelligence officer with an Arabic-speaking anthropologist. Analyzing social dynamics and how they relate to conflict often goes beyond the training of many military members and is indeed a challenge to the most experienced social scientists. In such settings, the movement of goats into an area can be as much of a threat to a cease-fire as the movement of military forces. Goats in much of the Sudan use land in a nonsustainable manner, and this is not lost on cattle and camel pastoralists who often view goats as a threat to their own survival. Similarly, the arrival of pastoralists in some areas sparks conflict.

Monitors work with the groups that have agreed to the cease-fire. The JMC monitors in the Nuba Mountains were tasked with providing unbiased reporting to a commission composed of members of the SPLA, GOS, and the international community. Since the success of the cease-fire was based partially on accurate reporting across the spectrum of society, it was critical that methodologies were in place that accounted for all elements of the population. Skewed statistics would have been acquired if the monitors focused only on those who spoke English and were in proximity to roads. Additionally, the GOS and the SPLA routinely restricted the freedom of movement of local Sudanese, and translators very often could not be trusted. Consequently, it became important to walk to remote areas and interact without using translators.

It was through this type of active outreach that monitors could become aware of social conditions, attitudes, and recent violence. Not all acts of violence, though, were cease-fire violations. It took understanding of the operating environment to effectively differentiate how one killing is a violation and how another is not. In one case, a thirteen-year-old Nuban boy was shot and killed by a Baggara. This boy had been previously sold by his family to herd cows for the Baggara. The shooting was done by a teenager, possibly by accident and possibly as the result of a dispute. Our determination was that the shooting was not a cease-fire violation because it was not directly related to the conflict. In another incident that was a cease-fire violation, a forty-year-old Hawazma Baggara had been shot and killed, and the twenty-six goats he was herding had been stolen. It is noteworthy that our response team for this incident included our camp doctor, a German who specialized in human rights abuses. This allowed a forensic examination to be conducted and led to our strong hypothesis that his killers were affiliated with the SPLA and were using the conflict boundaries as a means to evade capture.

These cases typified the hybrid civil-military nature of problems that can be faced by cease-fire monitors. The Baggara was wearing a military uniform because he was a member of the Popular Defense Forces (PDF) and also because good-quality clothing was at a premium in that area. The PDF was a government militia of local residents involved in atrocities in the civilian populations of Kordofan and Darfur. The PDF, though, also provided security from bandits and the SPLA. In all likelihood, this was an act of banditry and not an SPLA-sanctioned killing or a revenge killing. Regardless, it was widely and realistically assumed that the individuals who killed him were off-duty members of the SPLA using weapons provided by the SPLA.

This incident threatened the cease-fire since members of the deceased individual's village were preparing to make retribution against the ethnic group they perceived to be responsible for the killing. Given that the ethnic groups on each side were also affiliated with armed military organizations, the civil aspects of this act became enmeshed in the military dimension. This fact was not lost on the GOS soldiers in the area and whose commander put his forces on a high state of alert and directed them to prevent any Baggara from carrying arms. This act also highlights the tensions that exist within the forces commonly affiliated with the government side. Rather than being a unified force, the Sudanese army and the Baggara often erupted in violence, even though they were ostensibly aligned. Whereas this might seem counterintuitive within a political-military analytical framework, it is obvious when examined on the basis of modes of livelihood, since government-owned mechanized farms interfered with cattle migration routes.

Land Mine Removal

As with cease-fire monitoring and peacekeeping, land mine removal is a socially complex activity that military units or individuals with military experience are often the most qualified to carry out. Military personnel trained in demining are greatly enhanced by individuals familiar with social dynamics and behavior. To begin with, one must have a strong idea of the location of mines and be able to prioritize the application of very limited mine removal assets. In the Nuba Mountains, it was common for SPLA engineers to lie about the locations of mines to preserve their land mine stock. Not only did this endanger monitors, it misdirected demining efforts. It was only after relations with the local populations were built that we gained better insight into actual locations of mines. Other considerations involve economic prioritizations of areas for mine removal and the method of mine detection. For example, the use of mine-sniffing dogs has met with mixed results in parts of the Middle East because of attitudes toward the animals, which often resulted in the substandard care and death of these expensive and highly trained canines.

The two other elements of US and international demining operations are victims' assistance and public awareness campaigns. With both of these activities, it is important to identify vulnerable populations such as refugees and displaced people who may be excluded from mainstream power structures. Mine awareness campaigns must also use appropriate languages delivered in effective media. In some parts of Africa, therefore, radio and television would be trumped by posters, skits, and songs delivered by highly mobile language-capable teams. Additionally, as the name implies, humanitarian demining must be done for the good of people and not to increase one side's military, political, or economic advantage over another. Such detailed understandings are difficult to gain by military members on short tours but are generally obvious to social scientists who have conducted field research in those areas.

Fighting Terrorism in Africa

In addition to peacekeeping and countering the threat posed to civilian populations by land mines, the US military is engaged in aid and economic development activities throughout much of Africa. The commander of AFRICOM describes these activities as being a form of *stability operations* (Ward 2009, 29), the current buzzword in the US military lexicon that lends an air of doctrinal justification to activities often perceived to be outside traditional military mission sets. Although they are referred to as humanitarian in nature, most military development activities are not humanitarian in the sense that they are not based solely on the needs of the population. Rather, populations are most often chosen because of a military interest in a particular group or region. This reason alone should be enough to discourage involvement by credible members of the academic community. Or should it? This assumes this is an intractable state of affairs not susceptible to change.

Much of US military involvement in Africa is planned, directed, and executed by individuals with no training in development work and no experience in Africa. The missions are often vague and the sustainment is limited because many of the people involved are assigned such duties only for a year before resuming their primary military duties on a ship, aircraft, or tank. As with demining, the successful drilling of wells and allocation of limited humanitarian assistance funds require more than just good intentions. They also require an understanding of developmental economics and the second- and third-order effects than can occur when social structure and the environment are altered. The results speak for themselves. US military development activities in Africa are marked by disproportionately high costs, inefficiency, and a notable lack of expertise (Brigety 2008, 5). In the absence of specialized skills and regional knowledge it is only logical that military activities have had limited success. Ironically, despite efforts to win hearts and minds, US civil-military assistance can actually have a net negative effect when done poorly. This is most often a product of creating unfulfilled expectations. Gaining expertise, however, takes time, and mistakes will be inevitable.

The effects can also be negative if military members are suspected of using humanitarian operations as a cover for intelligence collection and special operations, as is commonly perceived throughout much of Africa. The US military is operating along the coast of East Africa because this predominantly

Muslim area is presumed to be vulnerable to Islamic extremism. Labeling the area simply as Muslim or even Swahili, though, is inadequate. These are broad categorizations that mask a diversity of localized expressions and interpretations. Historically, Islam in this region has been as much (or more) of an economic and political force as it has been a set of cosmological beliefs. For example, the majority of rural adult Muslim residents in much of coastal Tanzania do not make a distinction between Shia and Sunni versions of Islam, and many are not aware of the political, social, or theological differences. Even the distinction between Islam and Christianity can be blurry in that part of Africa. Many Muslims in rural coastal areas, including Islamic clergy, say that Christianity and Islam are just different sects within the same religion. In practice, both religions are woven into a larger cloth of traditional religion that includes a belief in spirit possession, the power of ancestors, sacrifice, and the use of charms, potions, and magical powders. Conversions between Christianity and Islam (regardless of gender) are common, and Muslims and Christians engage in traditional religious practices together, including animal sacrifice and propitiation of ancestors at temples in the forest.

The discrediting of socialism and communism as viable practical ideologies to address social discontent has created new space for fundamentalist forms of Islam to resonate throughout the world. In the US military, this has been amplified to allow some to redirect their same efforts to a war on terror in place of a war on communism (in between we had to make do with a war on drugs). Like political ideologies, though, local performances of religion are tempered by cultural consciousness and not necessarily linked to more orthodox performances seen elsewhere. Tying the rural coastal residents of Tanzania and Kenya to broader global religious flows thus has its limitations. True, many Swahili have strong and often polarized opinions on American involvement in Iraq, and some coastal smugglers use militarized Islam as a threatening facade to deter outsiders. However, rather than being enmeshed with global religious politics, rural coastal residents of Tanzania and Kenya are often focused more on local politics and life cycles.

With regard to the US global war on terror, accurate understandings provide a better framework for assessing populations vulnerable to extremist influences, why and under what conditions. Just as important, US military leaders can steer away from counterterrorism activities in areas where it is inappropriate. Here it is necessary for military leaders to understand the operational contexts and the image thresholds of multiple identities. Image threshold refers to appearances of conformity for elements of ethnicity that cannot be compromised. Religion, for example, may be practiced in localized forms, but there are still lines that cannot be crossed. There may be propitiation of spirits, but this may be done in an Islamic paradigm, which does not undermine the existence of Allah or God. Similarly, certain rituals may be performed in secrecy or orchestrated in a new syncretic form. In much of coastal Tanzania, protective amulets known as *herizi* are worn concealed. One rationale for this is that their protective powers are enhanced when they are kept secret. Another more functional explanation, though, is that they signify too much of a public deviance from Islam. Also, to address this, some herizi combine traditional magical components with passages from the Koran or with chalk dust that comes from erasing Koranic passages from blackboards in schools.

Julius Nyerere, the first president of Tanzania, implemented Swahili as a unifying national language. In addition to being a language, Swahili refers to a geographically and religiously defined ethnic group. Many of the historical slave traders in East Africa were Swahili, and individuals and groups adopted Swahili identity as a means of protection against slavery. This very often included visible conversion to Islam and directly supporting the slave trade, most commonly through providing labor for the massive slave caravans that ventured deep into the African interior. Consequently, Swahili culture is broad and includes multiple ethnotribal groups, with the inland residents of the same descent groups often not considering themselves to be Swahili. While much of the inland population has embraced Christianity to a certain degree, Islamic culture and cultural practices are an integral element of Swahili ethnic identity (Mazrui and Shariff 1994, 34). It is partly this distinction between Islam as a cultural identity and Islam as a purely religious institution that results in flexible and situational identities and defies categorizations made solely on the basis of demographics.

As in Sudan a competition for ideological control of Islam as a political, economic, and religious force also exists in Tanzania. Far from being seen as the ideal performance of Islam, the Arab form of the religion is often seen as foreign and contrary to the interests of coastal Tanzanians. It is recognized that Islam originated from the Arabian Peninsula, that Arabic is a sacred script, and that the hajj is a pillar of the faith. However, religious leadership is exclusively local, most often hereditary and integrated with traditional religious practices. For instance, village religious leaders are very often also traditional healers who engage in forms of sacrifice, magic, and ancestor worship. In this sense, the traditional religious leadership of villages was not displaced by Islam. Rather, traditional religious leaders incorporated it and took control of it under their own terms to not disrupt the status quo. As one example, Arab spirits are viewed by many local residents as malign and attempting to gain a foothold in the area.

The actions of village Imams and traditional healers therefore center on countering their presumed influence.

This symbolic opposition to Arab influences at once reinforces local control of religion and defines the group in relation to others. This theme is also reflected linguistically, and individual usages of words can reflect self-definitions of ethnicity. As a case in point, the Arabic word *Allah* and the Bantu word *Mungu* in Swahili refer to the same divine entity, God. However, the words are not always interchangeable. This is revealed when an outsider is corrected for using Allah instead of Mungu, or vice versa. Such indicators are admittedly difficult to integrate into strategic analysis and operational planning. Indeed, the units of analysis inherent in anthropology discourage strategic approaches to understanding culture. Yet they are an important, if nuanced, element in understanding operating environments and effectively interacting with local residents.

Sudanese in the Nuba Mountains did not have the same options in negotiating their own expressions of Islam. The conflict and the threat of violence were imposed externally and provided a limited array of adaptive strategies. Indeed, the desired uniformity of Islam by government forces accounts for "impious" Muslims' being targeted as much as nonbelievers. In the absence of such violent coercive measures, effective political efforts to unify peoples and define them in relation to others must accommodate the integrated elements of ethnicity. Religion here is but one element of an identity that also includes political, linguistic, social, and economic factors. While this alone is not indicative of a lack of religious conviction, it demonstrates that the effective instrumentality of religion combines enlightened self-interest with acceptable and relevant authenticating ideologies. As a case in point, Islam has been most successful in East Africa when it has been accompanied by social services such as education and medical care.

In this vein, those who advocate US hearts-and-minds efforts must understand and account for how religion is nested in the socioeconomic structure. In another case, residents of a fishing village warned me that their village was filled with "devout Muslims" who opposed the United States. Because I was American, they would not guarantee my safety and said it was too dangerous for me to visit. After several months of my living in the area, however, it became evident there was very limited applied religious sentiment in that village. On the contrary, the village was the area's center for smuggling timber, poached meat, and drugs. The warning had nothing to do with the United States or Islam. Instead, it was an attempt to manipulate these symbols to limit observation of smuggling. Once I had established relations in the area, particularly with the poachers who traded there, I was welcome in the village. Ironically, such a ploy is more likely to invite unwanted US attention than to deter it. US civil assistance efforts would be perceived to undermine local informal economies and result in negative attitudes toward the United States. This would likely be magnified if the civil assistance efforts were accompanied by intelligence or special operations personnel intending to infiltrate local smuggling activities, which are viewed in the US military as being susceptible for dual use by terrorists.

The rich cultural variance of East Africa goes beyond religion. Cultural influences are historically derived from Swahili, Bantu, Nilotic, European, and Asian groups, as well as over several hundred different linguistic-tribal groupings. In spite of this heterogeneity, Tanzania also provides a case study on the integration of a strong civil-national component into the ethnic mix. Far from being a tribal society, Tanzania has a strong civil identity that manifests itself in social structure and relations. Much of this stems from postcolonial history. To avert tribalism and ethnopolitical stratification at the time of independence, President Nyerere attempted to create national and civil identities that transcended ethnic and tribal loyalties. His largely successful efforts account for many of the contemporary political differences between Tanzania and neighboring Kenya, where tribal identities and patrimonial relations continue to define much of the political landscape. Consequently, Americans in Tanzania are counterproductive when attempting to interact with stereotypical tribal leaders, despite our repeated efforts to do so and the willingness of many individuals to volunteer as tribal power brokers. In Kenya, though, an understanding of the relationships between tribal and government leaders is essential.

Academic and Military Interactions

The thought of an American empire is rightfully distasteful to many Americans and non-Americans alike. The US invasion of Iraq symbolized a willingness and desire of some Americans to use military force to subdue those who do not submit to US power. In this setting, many American scholars have distanced themselves from the military apparatus that is acting in their name. The halcyon days of American military and political leaders' talking of permanent bases in Iraq and using that country as a platform to spread democracy and free markets throughout the Middle East, though, have thankfully given way to US military withdrawal. Iraq has highlighted not only the utter devastation that is inherent in social collapse, it has also shown the US military's limitations in effectively operating in complex environments. Nevertheless, US political, economic, and military involvement throughout the world is a fact that is unlikely to change in the foreseeable future. Wars will also continue, some involving the United States and others not.

Marvin Harris (1974, 250) describes a technocrat as a "heartless, inscrutable technician devoted to expert knowledge, but indifferent as to who uses it and for what end." This is exactly what members of the academic community working with the military cannot be and what they must strive to prevent soldiers from becoming. Scholars can provide insight and guidance to military leadership as a way of tempering the inefficiency and often inappropriate levels of violence and firepower that characterize US military operations throughout the world. Through teaching and direct involvement, knowledgeable academics can attempt to sensitize military leaders to some of the costs and benefits associated with potentially shortsighted or harmful operations. Such involvement by social scientists should not be equated to moral approval of US operations. Nor should academic relations with the military result in the subordination or compromise of scholarship to meet the demands of a military chain of command. Scholars involved with military activities must be buffered from the short-term institutional demands that characterize many military units and missions. In this sense, scholars working with the military can hold the military externally accountable while counterbalancing groupthink and inexperienced chains of command.

Relations between the academic community and the military will never be a Panglossian situation in which social scientists can save the day and make everyone's life better. Nor should they. As with the US military's so-called "humanitarian operations," social science research is subject to manipulation and misuse (Varhola and Varhola 2006, 76). Many in the military would attempt to use civilian anthropologists and social scientists as a cover to conduct intelligence activities and special operations (Ricks 2006, 166). This highlights the lack of understanding and perspective of many senior American military leaders. In the case of AFRICOM, the SSRC adheres to strict ethical guidelines and restrictions that include informed consent, transparency of funding sources, and disclosure of research scope and purpose. In principle, such guidelines can be likened to those already in place for doctors, lawyers, and chaplains in military service. Whereas we espouse a principle of do no harm, this is a problem for all members of the academic community, because doing nothing may be more harmful than doing something.

The paradox rests with the complexity of situations that makes the contributions of social scientists so valuable. This is particularly evident in Africa. Jomo Kenyatta's (1965) *Facing Mount Kenya* is as much a political construction of identity and anticolonial treatise as it is an ethnography of the Kikuyu. Later, as president of Kenya, Kenyatta was masterful at manipulating ethnic identity to maintain his hold on power. Similarly, the senior leadership of the Sudan liberation movement and the Justice and Equality Movement in Darfur include Sudanese anthropologists who recognize the inevitability and effectiveness of instrumentalizing ethnicity in conflict (DeWaal and Flint 2005, 81, 89). Anthropologists in AFRICOM SSRC strive to not be placed in such categories but at the same time take an active role in attempting to improve US military decision making in Africa.

Conclusion

The need for peacekeeping and the challenges inherent in protecting growing civilian populations throughout the world is likely to increase. Failure in these endeavors can have long-term catastrophic and cyclical impacts. The US expedition to Somalia not only contributed to social collapse in that country, it influenced the unwillingness of the United States to intervene in the genocide in Rwanda. The legacy is arguably still seen in the United States' unwillingness to involve itself in the ongoing crisis in Darfur. Like in Somalia and Rwanda, effective military interventions in Darfur would require an applied understanding of ethnic and social dynamics that must be integrated into military operations in a rapid deployment sequence. Such integration is challenging, especially when done on an ad hoc basis and in the absence of experts in the military. Cultural and regional specialists in habitual relationships with the military are one way of offsetting some of the challenges.

The peacetime luxury and fiction of separating combat from stability operations has dissolved, but the institutional method used by the US military to address stability operations is still a work in progress. Those holding rank in the military are expected to be experts regardless of whether they have any training and experience in a given region. The results are superficial understandings that dogmatically become an institutionalized standard. Improvements have been made, and there is no shortage of analysis on the developments in civil-military training and understanding of Iraqi history and society in the years since the removal of Saddam Hussein. All services have improved training and education of service members to meet threats that at one point were considered unconventional, asymmetric, and less important than meeting enemy forces in imaginary set-piece engagements. The Marine Corps has its culture center focused on education and training and a related effort to integrate culture into intelligence, the Army has a center for cultural training in Arizona, the Navy has developed a Maritime Civil Affairs Group, and the Air Force has established its Culture and Language Center. Many other small programs and initiatives exist in the services and combatant commands. The AFRICOM SSRC is the latest complement to this growing focus and capability.

These organizations are only as good as their faculty and staff. The danger also exists that the emphasis on studying society and culture in the military might be a passing phase meant to meet immediate operational necessities. In future budget and manpower equations, it remains to be seen if regional analysis and training will once again be overshadowed by more conventional and quantifiable military priorities. The presence of an academic community, though, remains a constant in American society. Scholars are valuable national assets who can significantly influence their nation's military if given the opportunity to do so. However, it should always be noted that their military will act in their name and with the support of their tax dollars regardless of their involvement.

Author's Note

The views expressed in this work are the author's alone and do not represent the position of the US Army or Department of Defense.

7

Master Narratives, Retrospective Attribution, and Ritual Pollution in Anthropology's Engagements With the Military

Robert A. Rubinstein

In this concluding chapter Robert A. Rubinstein explores some of the disciplinary barriers that anthropologists studying or working for the military have encountered. He applies an anthropological perspective to this analysis to show how these barriers are created and can be overcome. He identifies four processes that create these barriers—the reproduction of master narratives that oversimplify anthropological practice, retrospective attribution, metonymic reduction, and ritual pollution. Rubinstein suggests that anthropologists can neither understand nor change military institutions so long as the discipline does not take the military as an object of serious study or does not treat working responsibly for military institutions as a legitimate professional career path.

In March 2011 Melissa Matthes, a civilian assistant professor at the US Coast Guard Academy, posted the following query to a Listserv focusing on the sociology of Islam: "Who are the Libyan rebels?"[1] Matthes reported, "Within hours a stream of e-mails began—not answering my question, but debating what the relationship should be between the list's members and the US military. . . . Indignant members of the e-mail list were suspicious that their knowledge, if shared with faculty members at the service academies, would be distorted, appropriated, or in some way used to promote agendas to which they are not sympathetic. Indeed, some junior scholars worried in offline correspondence that communications with me could jeopardize their careers" (Matthes 2011, B4).

Matthes's experience is remarkably similar to our experiences in anthropology, like the 2007 incident where anthropologists working with military education institutions were called war criminals during the annual business meeting of the American Anthropological Association (AAA), mentioned in the preface of this volume and discussed more fully in this chapter. She concluded, as did we, that part of the reason for this kind of reaction is a lack of grounded understanding on what military anthropologists actually do. Our desire to begin to fill in this picture led us to assemble the chapters in this volume. All the contributors to this book describe what they do on a day-to-day basis, the personal and professional trajectories that led them to this work, and they comment on some of the challenges and rewards they meet as a result.

Providing this kind of grounded and forthright information about what it is like to work as a professional anthropologist in military settings is instructive on many levels. We hope the chapters will serve as a source of data that will mitigate otherwise free-floating and often erroneous assumptions. The contributions to this book may also show students contemplating anthropological careers something more about what they might expect to encounter if they were to follow working with the military as a professional path.

We are cognizant, however, that the kinds of ideologically driven responses we encountered in 2007 and that Matthes reports (see also McNamara and Rubinstein 2011; Lucas 2009) continue to dominate anthropological discussions of and reactions to the idea of anthropologists working with the military. That this framing of discussions of anthropology and the military persists among anthropologists, who in theory are engaged in exploring deeply and fairly ideas and practices they themselves may not want to do or share, suggests a need for an anthropologically reflexive commentary on why this is so.[2]

This chapter is a reflection on conversations about whether and how anthropology and anthropologists ought to engage with the military, security, and intelligence communities in the United States. It serves as a commentary on some of the characteristics of these discussions. My observations are based on my own extensive ethnographic work with the military and security community, especially relating to peacekeeping, my experiences talking about this work within anthropology, and published literature. It is useful to highlight at the outset the four main points of this chapter.

1. Master narratives have emerged in anthropology that give license to treating the military and military anthropologists in a totalizing fashion that our discipline would never sanction were they to be applied to other peoples.
2. These master narratives are constructed through a process of retrospective attribution in which the accuracy of a particular narrative account depends on discursive repetition rather than on empirical analysis.
3. These narratives create a kind of metonymic reduction in which particular, often extreme, aspects of some of the empirical phenomena do not just stand for the whole but are used to elide the heterogeneities and complexities that exist in the military and among military anthropologists.
4. Finally, I contend that all these processes lead many anthropologists to see engagement with the military as deeply polluting in ways that Mary Douglas's (1966) work helps render understandable.

I want to emphasize that I recognize there are many voices in this conversation and that they have a wide variety of perspectives and positions. Those I address here seem to me the normatively dominant ones, however. Without taking a position about the ultimate outcome of these conversations, it is my view that for anthropology a discussion of the meaning of engaging the military requires confronting these issues.

Master Narratives in Anthropology

Many of the shared conceptions of their discipline held by anthropologists often turn the just-so stories we tell one another into master narratives that organize, generate, and define the history and purposes of anthropology (Rubinstein 2002). These narratives use "a single voice that does not problematize diversity . . . [and] speaks unconsciously from the presumed center of things" (Star 1999, 384). Many of these master narratives often turn out to be partial or false when they are evaluated in the context of detailed historical accounts. Nevertheless, these narratives underwrite and shape the central conceptions of the discipline by organizing thinking about what anthropology is and what it does. By being reproduced in history texts and in our introductory textbooks they form for contemporary anthropology what Thomas Kuhn (1970, 182) referred to as the "disciplinary matrix." As described by Kuhn, the disciplinary matrix has four elements: (1) symbolic generalizations, which are the theories or laws propounded by scientific disciplines (182); (2) metaphysical models, which Kuhn describes as beliefs in heuristic models (184); (3) values that include articulating the preferred disciplinary approach (184–85); and (4) exemplars, concrete problem solutions students study in their texts and which teach them how to define and approach problems (186–87).

These narratives provide an uncluttered view of anthropology's history. The same applies in anthropological encounters with the military, security, and intelligence communities. But in so doing they allow for and even encourage thinking that is essentializing and totalizing in a way that most anthropologists would reject when speaking about any other people (for example, see the presentation in Gusterson 2007).

Discussions of the challenges (and dangers) for anthropology in engaging with the military are made by reference to narratives of earlier encounters, and these narratives include similar political shadings. One such episode, the US Department of Defense's efforts to involve social science in the service of its work in Latin America, Project Camelot, plays an outsized role in these anthropological narratives. It is, for instance, referred to by the AAA's Commission on the Engagement of Anthropology with the US Security and Intelligence Communities as a kind of totemic fetish: "scandals like Project Camelot still loom enormously in the collective anthropological memory" (Peacock et al. 2007, 22; see also Wakin 1992), they say. Yet, with a single exception, anthropologists had no role in the project (Horowitz 1967).

How does a complex project, with exceptionally limited anthropological involvement, get converted into an exemplar of anthropology's moral failings? George Lucas (2009) asks this question and answers it by considering it in terms of a broader discussion of ethics in anthropology's encounter with the military. It is also instructive to see this development in anthropological perspective, as part of the ordinary, day-to-day (some would call them mundane or prosaic) sense-making activities of a discipline creating its own image.

I note that one of the master narratives current in contemporary anthropology is that anthropologists work with those "at the margins," following Malinowski's (1954, 92) legacy of giving up the comfortable "chair on the verandah of the missionary compound, Government station, or planter's bungalow." In the context of the discussion of anthropology and the military, this narrative is transformed into an ideological position that anthropologists have a special bond to those affected by state power. Historical analysis shows that the story is much more complicated; indeed, this master narrative transforms a methodological advance into an ideological program (Rubinstein 2011), a course of action that threatens the integrity of the discipline (see, e.g., Tomforde 2011).

Retrospective Attribution

Writing about the development of scientific disciplines, Bruno Latour (1987) noted that the accepted truth of some claims often depends on what later observers say about them. He calls this process *retrospective attribution* and says: "The status of a statement depends on later statements. It is made more or less of a certainty depending on the next sentence that takes it up; this retrospective attribution is repeated for the next new sentence, which in turn might be made more of a fact or of a fiction by a third and so on" (27–28).

As I noted earlier, the master narratives in anthropology not only establish what is taken as conventionally true but can also introduce an ideological shading to these conversations. We can trace how some accounts get repeated, privileged, and naturalized in anthropology's disciplinary discourse with careful historical analysis. One can see how claims about a particular work may become detached from the substance of that work. In so doing the later claims present an incomplete or incorrect version of the original, which then becomes part of the received view in a discipline (see, for example, the discussion in Daubenmier 2008).[3]

Historical analysis can be a corrective. But in the era of Internet publication and blogging, it is also possible to observe the beginnings of this process. The following is an example relating the work of one of the coeditors of this volume, Kerry Fosher. (I choose this particular case mainly because it is so clear, and because it also helps later to illustrate the operation of metonymic reduction and ritual pollution in anthropology's engagement with the military.)

The University of Chicago Press published Kerry Fosher's (2009a) ethnographic account of how first responders in Boston construct conceptions of security. The book, *Under Construction: Making Homeland Security at the Local Level*, employs an ethnographic framework to trace and describe the day-to-day activities of this community and interprets them using anthropological theories.

Whether this book is a good ethnography or not is beside the point for my purposes here. What is important are the following seven points of background information:

1. *Under Construction* is a revision and expansion of Fosher's doctoral dissertation.

2. Her research was funded by the National Science Foundation and a variety of graduate research support grants offered by her university.
3. During her research, Fosher was affiliated with Syracuse University and a research center at Harvard University.
4. Her dissertation received an Outstanding Dissertation Award from the Syracuse University Graduate School. That award was made in open competition and determined through an interdisciplinary selection process.
5. Subsequently, Fosher worked for the New England Center for Emergency Preparedness at Dartmouth Medical School.
6. She then became the first command social scientist at the Marine Corp Intelligence Activity, which is the affiliation she gives in the book.
7. Fosher served on the AAA Commission on the Engagement of Anthropology with the US Security and Intelligence Communities.

With this background in mind, here are some excerpts from a review of this book by Jeremy Keenan (2009b), School of Oriental and African Studies, University of London. It is worth quoting the review at some length, so one can make a fair assessment of its tone and substance.

Keenan writes, "What is a 'security anthropologist'? I am not sure I know, except that Kerry Fosher, author of *Under Construction*, calls herself one. Fosher is the US Marine Corps' command social scientist at the Marine Corps Base at Quantico, Virginia. What, one might ask, is a 'command' social scientist? One who salutes before interviewing, or lets the interviewee 'stand easy.'"

In a paragraph largely reworked from the book's back cover, he goes on to say:

Fosher began an anthropological study of counterterrorism in Boston shortly before the 9/11 attacks. She thus found herself in the unique position of being able to observe the "construction" of "homeland security" in a major US metropolitan area in the immediate aftermath of 9/11, when security became the paramount concern of virtually everyone involved in governing the US. Her study of the development of the homeland security "community" in the Boston area is therefore unique.

But the bulk of his review offers the following:

> Imagine my surprise, on checking with the publisher, to learn that the book is an extensive revision, with new fieldwork, of the author's prize-winning dissertation. *While the American military-intelligence security establishment may well afford Fosher's work iconic status* [italics added], there are no such accolades from this reviewer: *Under Construction* is the epitome of all that anthropology should not be.
>
> The fundamental problem with her position, however, is that she seems to think that working in and for the military (albeit in a "corrective" position) can somehow be separated from its larger mission and project.
>
> That larger mission and project is one that has carried the greatest nation on earth (in the eyes of many) through the most shameful period in its history. It is the project of illegal invasion and occupation; of rendition and torture; of Abu Ghraib and Guantanamo; of complete disregard for international law, fundamental human rights and freedoms; of deception, disinformation, lies and dissemblement; of fabricated false flag terrorism incidents; and of killing and bringing suffering to tens of thousands of innocent peoples in the name of the global war on terror and in the cause of US imperialism.

I now turn to look critically at the substance of Keenan's review. There is no reasonable way to connect *Under Construction* with the work Fosher was doing at the time of publication; her dissertation research was carried out and written up before Fosher held the position that identified her in the book. If there is such a connection, rigorous scholarship would demand the link be demonstrated.[4]

Fosher's is not a study in counterterrorism. It is a study of the organization and conceptualization of disaster preparedness by people whose purpose is to aid and assist members of their community when a calamity—human or otherwise—puts them in mortal peril. Conflating emergency preparedness and counterterrorism as equivalents reveals an unconscionable lack of knowledge or a willful act of polemic on Keenan's part. Indeed, it would be like reviewing a book on aspects of life in a village whose members practice Sunni Islam and applying to it the theological and clerical structures of Shia Islam.

Keenan's assertion that Fosher's dissertation (and thus the subsequent book) received iconic status from the military intelligence security establishment is false. It creates the impression that the book and her Boston research is something other than what it was.

Finally, Keenan's long invective concerning US actions and policies calls into question whether he actually read the book he was reviewing. In my opinion, Keenan's review reflects, at best, lazy scholarship by someone who didn't make the effort for honest intellectual engagement.

In a sense Keenan's review is similar to many others in which the reviewer does not seem to apprehend what the book is about, and one should not take it especially seriously. Yet, that is precisely what the process of retrospective attribution depends on. Indeed, that process started almost immediately where Keenan's review is concerned. Returning to the *Times Higher Education* website where Keenan's review first appeared, we find a comment by Maximilian Forte (2009) that reads in part: "The much bigger problem is this, and the book seems to fall to pieces before it was even begun. . . . Such authors distort the conception of power to suit their career goals—they want to suck up to power, while pretending to speak truth to power. If you want to speak truth to power, position yourself in an Afghan wedding party during an American air raid, and then tell me about how power is managed and exercised. Thanks for the timely and well written warning about this book."

Although Keenan's presentation of the book he reviewed is largely detached from the substance of the book, the commentator accepts Keenan's inaccurate account without bothering to consult the text itself. Indeed, one can sense in the comment relief at having escaped the onus of actually looking at the book and making an informed judgment. We are witnessing the process of retrospective attribution in the making.

It might be objected that I am making too much of this review. It may be that Keenan's review is simply one of too many such examples of shoddy scholarship, written by an ideologue. Indeed that is one possibility. Even should that be the case, the process is still an invidious one that has damaging effects on anthropology as a discipline and on individual anthropologists. Let me illustrate.

Metonymic Reduction

To show why the process of retrospective attribution is so damaging, I return to the 2007 AAA annual meeting for a fuller account of the event that was one of the motivations for this book. Rubinstein and Fosher participated in the panel "The Empire Speaks Back: U.S. Military and Intelligence Organizations' Perspectives on Engagement with Anthropology" (Glenn 2007). I spoke about my work studying peacekeeping and how the obligations of reciprocity established with my informants led me to work with some of them to improve their practice in peacekeeping operations. I reported on my efforts in working with the United Nations, the US Army Peacekeeping Institute, the US Army War Colleges, the Joint Forces Staff College, predeployment training in negotiation at Fort Drum, and about a variety of encounters I had in classrooms and lecture halls. Others on the panel spoke about their efforts to introduce cultural understanding into the curricula of various professional military education settings.

The following day at the annual business meeting, a person rose from the floor to speak passionately against anthropology's engagement with the military. He said, "Yesterday there was a panel called 'The Empire Speaks Back.' Everyone on that panel is a war criminal, and should be banned from the association." (This quote is reconstructed, but the use of the term *war criminal* and the proposed banning of the panel participants are the speaker's own words.) There was applause at this remark. Charging anyone with being a war criminal, and proposing sanctions as a result, is a serious act. Yet no objections to this comment were made from the floor or from those presiding over the meeting.

When I raised the remark with colleagues after the meetings, the replies I got had two troubling themes.[5] The first, akin to the possible dismissing of the Keenan (2009b) review as simply poor scholarship that slipped by, was that the remark had been made by someone whom no one took seriously; "Oh, that was crazy old Harry; everybody knows he's way out there."[6] I for one did not know this, and so presumably neither did others in the room, the comment had been made publicly in a professional meeting attended by several hundred of our professional colleagues, and the meeting was public and open to the press. The second most common response was an equally troubling studied ignorance of the remark: "Oh, did someone say that? I didn't hear it; I must have been in a side conversation at the time."

After the meetings I learned of a conversation between two colleagues in which an interesting double standard emerged. The first colleague offered that the person making the war criminal comment had been behaving like a fascist. To this the second colleague quickly responded that we must be very careful about the accusations we make and the words we use; calling the speaker a fascist was going too far. Yet when then asked about the war criminal charge, the second colleague demurred, saying he would have to know more about it.

It is worth noting that none of the anthropologists on the panel had been involved in any kind of military operational role, nor had any of them supported combat operations. Rather they were speaking about acting as anthropologists educating the communities with which they work on questions of culture or conducting research on them. Some reported that in this context they had raised tough questions about how the military organizations they work with or study act. Nonetheless, "Harry's" remark glossed their work to a subset of military activity. At a minimum it creates a professional environment that is hostile and unwelcoming to the people involved in this work. It can also mark as out-of-bounds whole areas of investigation.

We know from studies of human cognition that people often think by analogy and employ conceptual metaphors to help them understand one domain of social life in terms of others they have experienced (Lakoff and Johnson 2003; Rubinstein, Laughlin, and McManus 1984). One of the strategies people use to do this is metonymy, where a part stands for the whole. Metonymy can be an expansive cognitive act that can structure a systematic and broader understanding of the target area of social life (Lakoff and Johnson 2003, 35–40).

In contrast, metonymy can also be used to reduce and misleadingly simplify the phenomenon under consideration. When a subset of the activity is taken as the whole (not just an avenue of cognitive access to the broader whole), or taken to be a much more substantial part of the activity than it actually is, the result limits rather than expands opportunities for investigation. Doing this leaves things out. This kind of elision is a metonymic reduction. Keenan's (2009b) review and "Harry's" accusations are examples of metonymic reduction.

One effect of these processes is that they put military anthropologists in a double bind. If on the one hand, they accede to the insistence that to be taken seriously they must speak about controversial programs like the Human Terrain System (HTS), then they find themselves constantly repeating their views on HTS and not being able to move to discuss the ethnographic data and conceptual materials they would like to address. In doing so, they reinforce the metonymic reduction and may be scolded for not contributing anything new ethnographically, which is then taken as evidence of the bankruptcy of their endeavors. On the other hand, if military anthropologists offer analyses of the things they find interesting and important and do not take HTS as their concern, they are accused of not participating in disciplinary discourses.

Ritual Pollution

Some time ago, I wrote, "Because of the suspicion with which anthropologists view the defense community, researchers risk being stigmatized because of those exchanges" (Rubinstein 2003, 24). Why should researchers working on aspects of a prominent set of institutions in our society fear that doing so will lead to their being ostracized from their discipline? It is not hard to see that the kinds sentiments expressed by the Keenan (2009b) review, Forte's (2009) response to it, and "Harry's" call give force to those concerns, especially since they are not exceptions, as Matthes reports.

There is, though, a more anthropological way to account for this. Keenan's (2009b) review and "Harry's" call are examples of people tending the boundaries of the discipline. Kerry Fosher (2009b) points out that "boundary tending is a legitimate exercise. However, the location of these boundaries and their permeability should be the subject of informed debate rather than polemics." In contrast, in their statements Keenan (2009b) and Forte (2009) articulate a conception of what anthropology ought to be and what it ought not be according to a particular ideological and polemic conception of the world. Both see the retrospectively, metonymically reduced acts of military anthropologists as profoundly threatening to the proper order of things anthropological. In short, they reinforce the master narratives they emerge from. And they are not alone.

Shortly after Seymour Hersh (2004) wrote in *The New Yorker* about the central role that Raphael Patai's *The Arab Mind* played in the Abu Ghraib torture, Laura McNamara was moved to ask an empirical question: what evidence was there that *The Arab Mind*, or anthropological literature more broadly, or individual anthropologists actually played a role in that episode? After a thorough search through thousands of pages of material obtained through the Freedom of Information Act, she found no evidence for this claim. Indeed, all paths led back to Hersh's original article (McNamara 2011). Yet her careful and transparent efforts were dismissed by the editor of *Anthropology Today*, based on nothing more than her affiliation—McNamara works for Sandia National Laboratories. In a move resonant with Keenan's (2009b) dismissal of Fosher's work because of her affiliation with the Marine Corps, he wrote:

> But why wait half a century before we can debate what McNamara and her secretive colleagues are up to *today*? Sandia National Laboratories, her employer, is managed and operated through a wholly

owned subsidiary of Lockheed Martin Corporation. . . . As a contractor responsible for military interrogation, Lockheed Martin was deeply involved in the torture and prisoner abuse scandals at Bagram and Abu Ghraib. . . . Two former presidents of her organization went on to work for Lockheed Martin, and one of the four current deputy directors also serves on a Lockheed Martin venture. One prominent advisor to her lab is separately associated with a different company, CACI International, at the heart of this scandal. . . . Given the close relationship between her laboratory and companies implicated in torture, can we fully trust her claim that anthropologists have no involvement in such practices? (Houtman 2007, 21)

One might ask on what basis do we trust any of the ethnographic or research reports of our colleagues? Anthropologists are notoriously secretive in their treatment of field notes. Indeed, the act of making our data available to other colleagues is the exception in anthropology rather than the rule.

Part of being human is to create categories that help regulate how we live, how we ought to behave, and separate what is good and desirable from what is not (Zerubavel 1993). In this context I am struck by the sense in Keenan's (2009b), "Harry's," and Houtman's (2007) comments that association with military anthropologists is profoundly polluting, and that there should be prohibitions against anthropologists engaging with the military in this way. Surely Mary Douglas (1966) would have recognized this process of articulating prohibitions as akin to her analyses of taboo and ritual impurity. I suspect that she would have seen in their comments both themes that emerged from her study. The prohibitions on anthropological engagement with the military that emerge from Keenan's, "Harry's," Houtman's, and others' similar comments serve as "device[s] for protecting the distinctive categories of the [anthropological] universe" and also provide a way of limiting "the cognitive discomfort cause by ambiguity" (Douglas 1966, xi).

Further, their discourse presumes a kind of moral purity, setting them apart and above the military anthropologists they critique. Laura McNamara suggests there is a presumption that particular locations in academia accord a kind of purity. I have noted elsewhere that many of these critics work for state institutions and conduct their research using state money and that they pay their taxes, thus implicating them in support of the structures they abhor and scold others for supporting. In this connection, it is worth noting there is considerable, though unintended, irony in Keenan's (2009b) savaging of Fosher for her institutional affiliations, as he is institutionally situated in the School of Oriental and African Studies, created and supported by British colonialism. Further complicating Keenan's own moral position, and by his own logic equally contaminating, he asserted during his talk at Syracuse University,

> I sit on the Foreign Office Committee for Intelligence, I also brief the State Department, I brief the Pentagon, so I actually know what these guys are talking about. . . . But, just so you know why I get there, there's a group in the State Department, Pentagon, who will not have briefings unless I'm invited. So you have this strange ritual every six months where I get an air ticket and I'm flown over to Washington. (Keenan 2009a)

Conclusion

Military, intelligence, and security institutions and the people who participate in them are prominent parts of our society. Those institutions are a way of providing defense for the state and for its citizens. There are many examples of the military carrying out policies set by the civilian leadership in the United States that are objectionable and doing so in ways that are shameful. Yet it seems unreasonable to me to think that anthropology is better off not dealing with the military. If we don't study the military ethnographically we will not understand it as a human institution, and we cannot affect change in those institutions without interacting with the people in them just as we would any other group. Likewise, treating anthropological colleagues who interact with those institutions and individuals as *a priori* polluting limits severely the value of what we can learn and what we can do to affect changes in policy and actions.

The creation of master narratives about the military and about military anthropologists through the process of retrospective attribution coupled with the metonymic reduction of those activities to the most extreme and complicit forms of engagement results in the construction of stereotypes that are dangerous for the military anthropologists. Those stereotypes energize notions of anthropological impurity that are dangerous for our discipline as well, since it denies us the nuanced and empirical information about major, powerful institutions we need if we wish to control rather than be controlled by the encounter with the military.

Lest I be guilty of the kind of totalizing and essentializing I critique in this chapter, I repeat what I said earlier. Within anthropology there are people who contribute serious, empirically based, ethnographically rich, and wide-ranging analyses while offering critical assessments of anthropology's engagement with the military. Examples of these voices include Roberto González's (2009) work on American counterinsurgency, David Price's (2008) historical analyses, Keith Brown's (Brown and Lutz 2007) work on grunt literature, and Matthew Guttman and Catherine Lutz's (2010) work on veterans of the Iraq war.

The danger for anthropology is that those who seek to make grounded, empirically informed evaluations of the merits and dangers of anthropology's engagement with the military will be shouted down by those who wish to reduce that encounter to an ideological duel.

Part of the force of culture comes from activities taking place outside our daily consciousness. When we analyze these processes and make their content evident, we can diminish their power and make alternative action possible (Foster 1990). We hope that exposing the processes I identify in this conclusion for further analysis and combining them with the ethnographically rich accounts offered by the contributors to this book will help create the context in which military anthropology can become a field of reasoned discussion and, for those whom it suits, a professionally legitimate career path.

Notes

1. An earlier version of some of the material in this chapter was presented in "Scholars, Security and Citizenship 2," (plenary session, Annual Meeting of the Society for Applied Anthropology, Santa Fe, NM, March 19 2009). I thank Kerry Fosher, Clementine Fujimura, Sandra D. Lane, and Laura McNamara for comments on this chapter.

2. I thank Jim Lance for this particular formulation of the issue.

3. Some might fault writers for relying on others' representations rather than consulting the original work. There are, however, pragmatic reasons that make such reliance on colleagues' claims necessary and even desirable. This reliance is very much a problem when representations are subject to ideological shading.

4. Another error in Keenan's review is this: after noting that Fosher is an associate of the Syracuse University Institute for National Security and Counterterrorism (INSCT; again not pertinent to the substance of *Under Construction*), Keenan says, "For readers not familiar with INSCT, check the website. After the martial music, its introductory video (www.exed.maxwell.syr.edu/exed/sites/nss) tells us that its national security studies program is open to civilian and military leaders. Yet 100 percent of the alumni mentioned in its latest alumni newsletter hold senior positions in the US Defence Department and associated intelligence services." Even a cursory effort reveals that the website he directs his readers to is not the INSCT website at all.

Despite Keenan's swagger in this review, during Keenan's visit to speak at the Maxwell School of Syracuse University, which was attended by the INSCT director, Keenan made no mention of his objections to the institute's work.

5. Although I was in the audience, I too did not object even though I was stunned and offended by this speech. The context in which the remark provoked applause and the fact that I was among those so charged would have made voicing an objection an uncomfortably self-interested act. Perhaps others who thought to object were constrained in similar ways.

6. "Harry" is a pseudonym.

References

Aginsky, B. W. 1942. "Social Science and the World Situation." *American Anthropologist* 44 (3): 521–25.
Albro, Robert, George Marcus, Laura McNamara, and Monica Schoch-Spana, eds. 2011. *Anthropologists in the SecurityScape: Ethics, Practice and Professional Identity*. Walnut Creek, CA: Left Coast Press.
Albro, Robert, James Peacock, Carolyn Fluehr-Lobban, Kerry Fosher, Laura McNamara, George Marcus, David Price, et al. 2009. *AAA Commission on the Engagement of Anthropology with the US Security and Intelligence Communities (CEAUSSIC): Final Report on The Army's Human Terrain System Proof of Concept Program*. Washington, DC: American Anthropological Association.
Allen, Andi, Gina Ladenheim, and Katie Stout. 2010. "Training Female Engagement Teams: Framework, Content Development, and Lessons Learned" (Reference No. 10414). Paper presented at the Interservice/Industry Training, Simulation and Education Conference, Orlando, FL, December 2.
American Anthropological Society. 2009. *Code of Ethics of the American Anthropological Association*. http://www.aaanet.org/issues/policy-advocacy/upload/AAA-Ethics-Code-2009.pdf
Brigety, Reuben E. II. 2008. *Humanity as a Weapon of War: Sustained Security and the Role of the U.S. Military*. Washington, DC: Center for American Progress.
Brown, Keith, and Catherine Lutz. 2007. "Grunt Lit: The Participant Observers of Empire." *American Ethnologist* 34 (2): 322–28.
Bunzel, Ruth, Anne Parsons, Margaret Mead, and Rhoda Metraux. 1964. "Anthropology and World Affairs as Seen by U.S.A. Associates 1: Report on Regional Conferences." *Current Anthropology* 5 (5): 430, 437–42.
Carroll, Lewis. 1960. *The Annotated Alice: Alice's Adventures in Wonderland and Through the Looking Glass*. With an introduction and notes by Martin Gardner. New York: Bramhall House.
Chief of Naval Operations. 2007. *U.S. Navy Language Skills, Regional Expertise and Cultural Awareness Strategy*. Washington, DC: Department of the Navy.
Creuziger, Clementine. 1996. *Childhood in Russia: Representations and Reality*. Lanham, MD: University Press of America.
Daubenmier, J. M. 2008. *The Meskwaki and Anthropologists: Action Anthropology Reconsidered*. Lincoln: University of Nebraska Press.

DeWaal, Alex, and Julie Flint. 2005. *Darfur: A Short History of a Long War*. London: Zed.
Douglas, Mary. 1966. *Purity and Danger: An Analysis of Pollution and Taboo*. London: Routledge & K. Paul.
———. 1986. *How Institutions Think*. Syracuse, NY: Syracuse University Press.
Eggan, Fred. 1942. "Annual Meeting, December 30, 9:00 AM." *American Anthropologist* 44 (1): 138–39.
Embree, J. F. 1945. "Applied Anthropology and Its Relationship to Anthropology." *American Anthropologist* 41 (4): 634–37.
Forte, Maximilian. 2009. Comment on Keenan, "Review of *Under Construction*," February 15. http://www.timeshighereducation.co.uk/story.asp?sectioncode=26&storycode=405203&c=1.
Fosher, Kerry. 2005. "'I'm Just Thinking Out Loud Here': Making United States Homeland Security at the Local Level." PhD diss., Syracuse University.
———. 2009a. *Under Construction: Making Homeland Security at the Local Level*. Chicago: University of Chicago Press.
———. 2009b. "Contributing to the Discipline: Considerations for Anthropologists Working with the Military." Panel presented at the meeting of the Society for Applied Anthropology, Sante Fe, NM, March.
———. 2010. "Yes, Both, Absolutely: A Personal and Professional Commentary on Anthropological Engagement with Military and Intelligence Organizations." In *Anthropology and Global Counter Insurgency*, edited by J. Kelly, B. Jauregui, S. Mitchell, and J. Walton, 261–71. Chicago: University of Chicago Press.
Fosher, Kerry, and Paul Nuti. 2007. "Reflecting Back on a Year of Debate with the Ad Hoc Commission." *Anthropology News* 48 (7): 3–4.
Foster, Mary LeCron. 1990. "Analogy, Language and the Symbolic Process." In *The Life of Symbols*, edited by Mary LeCron Foster and Lucy Jane Botscharow, 81–94. Boulder, CO: Westview Press.
Fujimura, Clementine. 2003. "Integrating diversity and understanding the other at the U.S. Naval Academy." In *Anthropology and the United States Military: Coming of Age in the Twenty-First Century*, edited by P. Frese and M. Harrell, 135–46. New York: Palgrave MacMillan.
———. 2005. *Russia's Abandoned Children: An Intimate Understanding*. New York: Praeger.
Glenn, David. 2007. "Report on How to Work with the Military Stirs Debate at Anthropologists' Meeting." *Chronicle of Higher Education*, November 30. http://chronicle.com/article/Report-on-Work-With-the/263.
González, Roberto. 2008. "From Anthropologists to Technicians of Power." Paper presented at the annual meeting of the Society for Applied Anthropology, Memphis, TN, March.
———. 2009a. *American Counterinsurgency: Human Science and the Human Terrain*. Chicago, IL: Prickly Paradigm Press.
———. 2009b. "A Phoenix Rising? The $60 Million U.S. Program to Embed Social Scientists in Combat Brigades." *Z Magazine*, May 1. http://www.zmag.org/zmag/viewArticlePrint/1750.
Guistozzi, Antonio, and Noor Allah. 2006. *"Tribes" and Warlords in Southern Afghanistan: 1980–2005*. London: Destin Studies Institute.
Gusterson, Hugh. 2007. "Anthropology and Militarism." *Annual Review of Anthropology* 36: 155–76.

Guttman, Matthew, and Catherine Lutz. 2010. *Breaking Ranks: Iraq Veterans Speak Out Against the War*. Berkeley: University of California Press.
Harris, Marvin. 1974. *Cows, Pigs, Wars and Witches: The Riddles of Culture*. New York: Vintage.
Henry, Jules. 1951. "National Character and War." *American Anthropologist* 53 (1): 134–35.
Hersh, Seymour M. 2004. "Annals of National Security: Torture at Abu Ghraib." *New Yorker*, May 10, 42–47.
Herskovits, Melville. 1945. "Anthropology during the War I." *American Anthropologist* 47 (4): 639–41.
Hickey, Gerald C. 2002. *Window on a War: An Anthropologist in the Vietnam Conflict*. Lubbock: Texas Tech University Press.
Holmes-Eber, Paula. 2003. *Daughters of Tunis: Women, Family and Networks in a Muslim City*. Boulder, CO: Westview Press.
———. 2011. "Teaching Culture at Marine Corps University." In *Anthropologists in the SecurityScape: Ethics, Practice and Professional Identity*, edited by R. Albro, G. Marcus, L. McNamara, and M. Schoch-Spana, 129–42. Walnut Creek, CA: Left Coast Press.
Horowitz, I. L. 1967. *The Rise and Fall of Project Camelot: Studies in the Relationship Between Social Science and Practical Politics*. Cambridge, MA: MIT Press.
Houtman, Gustaaf. 2007. "Gustaaf Houtman Responds." *Anthropology Today* 23 (2): 21.
Johnston, Rob. 2005. *Analytic Culture in the US Intelligence Community: An Ethnographic Study*. Washington, DC: Center for the Study of Intelligence, Central Intelligence Agency.
Jorgensen, Joseph G., and Eric Wolf. 1970. "Anthropology on the Warpath in Thailand." *New York Review of Books* 15 (9): 27–35. http://www.nybooks.com/articles/archives/1970/nov/1919/a-special-supplement-anthropology-on-the-warpath-i/, July 2010.
Keenan, J. 2009a. "Focus on the Fabrication of Terrorism in Algeria and Somalia" (speech). Syracuse University, Africa Initiative, February 19.
———. 2009b. Review of *Under Construction: Making Homeland Security at the Local Level: Where Ethics and Politics Intertwine* by Kerry B. Fosher. *Times Higher Education*, January 29. http://www.timeshighereducation.co.uk/story.asp?sectioncode=26&storycode=405203&c=1.
Kelly, John, Beatrice Jauregui, Sean Mitchell, and Jeremy Walton, eds. 2010. *Anthropology and Global Counter Insurgency*. Chicago: University of Chicago Press.
Kenyatta, Jomo. 1965. *Facing Mount Kenya*. New York: Random House.
Krulak, Victor H. 1991. *First to Fight: An Inside View of the U.S. Marine Corps*. New York: Simon & Schuster.
Kuhn, T. 1970. *The Structure of Scientific Revolutions*. Chicago: University of Chicago Press.
Lakoff, George, and Mark Johnson. 2003. *Metaphors We Live By*. Chicago: University of Chicago Press.
Latour, Bruno. 1987. *Science in Action: How to Follow Scientists and Engineers through Society*. Cambridge, MA: Harvard University Press.
Lucas, George. 2009. *Anthropologists in Arms: The Ethics of Military Anthropology*. Lanham, MD: Alta Mira Press.
Malinowski, B. 1954. *Magic, Science and Religion and other Essays*. With an Introduction by Robert Redfield. Garden City, NY: Doubleday.
Manger, Leif. 1994. *From the Mountains to the Plains: The Integration of the Lafofa Nuba into Sudanese Society*. Uppsala, Sweden: Scandinavian Institute of African Studies.
Matthes, Melissa. 2011. "It's Time for a Scholarly Truce with Military Academies." *Chronicle of Higher Education* 58 (8): B4–B5.

Mazrui, Alamin, and Ibrahim Noor Shariff. 1994. *The Swahili: Idiom and Identity of an African People*. Trenton, NJ: Africa World Press.

McNamara, Laura. 2011. "Torture Is for the Incompetent: Toward the Ethnography of Interrogation." In *Dangerous Liaisons: Anthropologists and the National Security State*, edited by Laura McNamara and Robert A. Rubinstein, 25–49. Santa Fe, NM: SAR Press.

McNamara, Laura, and Robert A. Rubinstein, eds. 2011. *Dangerous Liaisons: Anthropologists and the National Security State*. Santa Fe, NM: SAR Press.

Moon, Dreama. 2002. "Thinking about 'Culture' in Intercultural Communication." In *Readings in Intercultural Communication: Experiences and Contexts*, 2nd ed., edited by J. N. Martin, T. K. Nakayama, and L. A. Flores, 13–20. New York: McGraw Hill.

Peacock, James, Robert Albro, Carolyn Fluehr-Lobban, Kerry Fosher, Laura McNamara, Monica Heller, George Marcus, David Price, and Alan Goodman. 2007. *AAA Commission on the Engagement of Anthropology with the US Security and Intelligence Communities, Final Report*. Washington, DC: American Anthropological Association.

Price, David. 2008. *Anthropology and Intelligence: The Development and Neglect of American Anthropology in the Second World War*. Durham, NC: Duke University Press.

Ricks, Thomas. 2006. *Fiasco: The American Military Adventure in Iraq*. New York: Penguin Press.

Rubinstein, Robert A., ed. 2002. *Doing Fieldwork: The Correspondence of Robert Redfield and Sol Tax*. New Brunswick, NJ: Transaction.

———. 2003. "Politics and Peacekeepers: Experience and Political Representation among United States Military Officers." In *Anthropology and the United States Military: Coming of Age in the Twenty-First Century*, edited by Pamela R. Frese and Margaret C. Harrell, 15–27. New York: Palgrave Macmillan.

———. 2008. *Peacekeeping under Fire: Culture and Intervention*. Boulder, CO: Paradigm.

———. 2011. "Ethics, Engagement, and Experience: Anthropological Excursions in Culture and the National Security State." In *Dangerous Liaisons: Anthropologists and the National Security State*, edited by Laura McNamara and Robert A. Rubinstein, 145–65. Santa Fe, NM: SAR Press.

Rubinstein, Robert A., Charles D. Laughlin, and John McManus. 1984. *Science as Cognitive Process: Toward an Empirical Philosophy of Science*. Philadelphia: University of Pennsylvania Press.

Rush, Laurie, ed. 2010. *Archaeology, Cultural Property, and the Military*. Rochester, NY: Boydell Press.

Salmoni, Barak, and Paula Holmes-Eber. 2011. *Operational Culture for the Warfighter: Principles and Applications*, 2nd ed. Quantico, VA: Marine Corps University Press.

Samoff, Joel. 1982. "Pluralism and Conflict in Africa: Ethnicity, Interests and Class in Africa." Paper presented at the International Political Science Association World Congress, Rio de Janeiro, Brazil, August.

Small, Cathy. 2008. "Applying Anthropology to Teaching Anthropology." *General Anthropology* 15 (1): 1–4.

Star, Susan Leigh. 1999. "The Ethnography of Infrastructure." *American Behavioral Scientist* 43 (3): 377–91.

Tomforde, Maren. 2011. "Should Anthropologists Provide Their Knowledge to the Military? An Ethical Discourse Taking Germany as an Example." In *Dangerous Liaisons: Anthropologists and the National Security State*, edited by Laura McNamara and Robert A. Rubinstein, 77–100. Santa Fe, NM: SAR Press.

Turnley, Jessica. 2006. *Implications for Network-Centric Warfare*. JSOU Report 06-3 March 2006. Hurlburt Field, FL: Joint Special Operations University Press. http://www.dtic.mil/cgi-bin/GetTRDoc?Location=U2&doc=GetTRDoc.pdf&AD=ADA495530.

———. 2008. *Retaining a Precarious Value as Special Operations Go Mainstream*. JSOU Report 08-2 February 2008. Hurlburt Field, FL: Joint Special Operations University Press. http://www.dtic.mil/cgi-bin/GetTRDoc?Location=U2&doc=GetTRDoc.pdf&AD=ADA495335.

US Department of Defense. 2011. *Strategic Plan for Language Skills, Regional Expertise and Cultural Capabilities 2011–2016*. Washington, DC: US Department of Defense.

US Special Operations Command. 2010. *USSOCOM Fact Book*. http://www.socom.mil/News/Documents/USSOCOMFactBook2011.pdf.

Varhola, Christopher. 2007. "Cows, Korans, and Kalashnikovs: The Multiple Dimensions of Conflict in the Nuba Mountains." *Military Review* 87 (May–June): 46–55.

Varhola, Christopher, and Laura R. Varhola. 2006. "Defense Diplomacy in East Africa: The Cookie Cutter Approach to Culture." *Military Review* 86 (November–December): 73–78.

Wakin, Eric. 1992. *Anthropology Goes to War*. Madison: University of Wisconsin Press.

Ward, William "Kip" E. 2009. "Operationalizing FM 3-07 Stability Operations in U.S. Africa Command." *Army Magazine* 59 (2): 28–34.

Wolfe, Robert P. 1963. "Report of Replies to the Invitation to a Conference on Anthropology and World Affairs." Unpublished manuscript.

Zerubavel, Eviatar. 1993. *The Fine Line: Making Distinctions in Everyday Life*. Chicago: University of Chicago Press.

Editors and Contributors

Kerry Fosher is director of research at the US Marine Corps Center for Advanced Operational Culture Learning. From 2007 until 2010, Fosher worked as the command social scientist for the US Marine Corps Intelligence Activity. Prior to her work with the Marine Corps, Fosher was a research assistant professor with the New England Center for Emergency Preparedness at Dartmouth Medical School. Fosher received her PhD in cultural anthropology from Syracuse University. Her publications include *Under Construction: Making Homeland Security at the Local Level* (2008) as well as a number of articles and reviews.

Clementine Fujimura is professor of anthropology and Russian in the Languages and Cultures Department at the US Naval Academy. Fujimura researches and publishes on the subject of teaching culture and languages in a military environment and the role of anthropology in military education while continuing her research on orphans and adoptive families in the United States and Russia. Fujimura is the only full professor of anthropology at the academy, and while teaching courses in Russian and German languages, cultures, and literatures, she also teaches cultural anthropology and intercultural communication. In 2006 Fujimura was the recipient of the Civilian Faculty Teaching Excellence Award at the academy. She was selected as a Stockdale Fellow in 2007–2008 to continue this research for the Navy. Fujimura has presented her work to the Chief of Naval Operations Strategic Studies Group, the Elliot School of International Relations, the Watson Institute, and at a number of conferences, panel discussions, and invited lecture series. She is currently coeditor of the journal *Health, Science and the Humanities*. Fujimura received her PhD from the University of Chicago in cultural anthropology and published her dissertation "Childhood in Russia: Representation and Reality" (née Creuziger) in

1996. Her research next developed into a study on child abandonment, children's rights, and ethnic marginalization in Russia and former Soviet republics. She received a Title VIII fellowship from the Kennan Institute in 1997 and spent two years (1999–2001) in Moscow conducting fieldwork on the subject of homeless children. Articles on the subject have appeared in journals such as *Childhood* and *The Anthropology of East Europe Review,* and *Demoktratizatsiya.* She published her second book, *Russia's Abandoned Children: An Intimate Understanding,* in 2005.

Paula Holmes-Eber is a professor of operational culture at Marine Corps University. She also supports the Center for Advanced Operational Culture Learning on academic matters concerning culture, Islam, Arab society, and North Africa. She received her PhD from Northwestern University. Her research and expertise focus on kinship and social networks in Arab and Muslim culture in North Africa. Prior to her current position, Paula was an assistant professor of anthropology at the University of Wisconsin–Milwaukee and a visiting scholar in the Middle East Center at the Jackson School of International Studies at the University of Washington. Holmes-Eber's publications include *Applications in Operational Culture: Perspectives from the Field* (2009), cowritten with Patrice Scanlon and Andrea Hamlen; *Operational Culture for the Warfighter: Principles and Applications* by Barak Salmoni and Paula Holmes-Eber (2008, 2011), and *Daughters of Tunis: Women, Family and Networks in a Muslim City* (2003). She is the author of several entries in the *Encyclopedia of Women and Islam* and has published a number of articles for and on the Marine Corps.

Robert A. Rubinstein is professor of anthropology and international relations at the Maxwell School of Citizenship and Public Affairs, Syracuse University. His work focuses on political anthropology, medical anthropology, and history and theory in anthropology. He conducts empirical research on multilateral peacekeeping, the dynamics of post-conflict societies, on health and conflict, and on health disparities. He received a PhD in anthropology from State University of New York Binghamton, and an MsPH from the University of Illinois School of Public Health. He has published extensively in journals and has written several books. He is author of *Peacekeeping Under Fire: Culture and Intervention* (2008), and coeditor with Laura McNamara of *Dangerous Liaisons: Anthropologists and the National Security State* (2011).

Laurie W. Rush is the director of the Office of the Secretary of Defense Legacy Project, which is called "In Theater Heritage Training Program for Deploying

Personnel," and is the cultural resources manager at Fort Drum, New York. Rush helped to establish a partnership between the Archaeology Institute of America and the Department of Defense. She is also working toward improved archaeology mapping for military planning and military guidelines for stability operations in archaeologically sensitive areas. Rush received her PhD from Northwestern University where she was a fellow of the University and of the National Science Foundation. She moved to northern New York in 1983 and has been doing museum and archaeological work in the area ever since. She was assistant director of the Antique Boat Museum in Clayton, NY, in the 1980s, set up the archaeology curation facility at Fort Drum from 1992 to 1994, and has been managing the Fort Drum cultural resources program since the fall of 1998. In 2009 Major General Michael Oates, commander of the US Army Tenth Mountain Division, requested that Rush serve as the military liaison for the successful return of the Ancient City of Ur to Iraqi stewardship. In 2010 Rush traveled to Kabul with US Central Command personnel to participate in environmental *shuras* (consultations) and to meet with the director general of heritage for the Islamic Republic of Afghanistan and US State Department officials to establish increased awareness and military partnership for preservation projects in Kabul and Mes Aynak. Rush is editor of *Archaeology, Cultural Property, and the Military* (2010).

Jessica Glicken Turnley is president of Galisteo Consulting Group in Albuquerque, NM. She also holds an appointment as senior fellow, Joint Special Operations University, US Special Operations Command. Turnley's current work includes several projects focused on the social and cultural aspects of homeland security, the assessment of the terrorist threat, and the critical assessment of our own national security complex. She has served on the Defense Intelligence Agency Advisory Board. She also is working in the area of the social study of science. Other projects include providing support to the Environmental Protection Agency in the development of approaches to assess social, cultural, and economic impacts at Superfund sites, establishing a binational applied research laboratory with Mexico, and research in the cultural aspects of workplace safety. Prior to Galisteo, Turnley worked for ecological planning and toxicology focusing on risk communication and stakeholder involvement in public decision making. In this capacity she has conducted workshops in China and Poland on citizen involvement and participated in efforts to formalize public participation in environmental management in the United States. Turnley has also served as a technical manager at Sandia National Laboratories and has worked in the nonprofit world. Turnley has a PhD in cultural anthropology/

Southeast Asian Studies from Cornell University. She has published numerous articles on subjects such as computational social models, knowledge production, and protected spaces.

Christopher Varhola was the first director of the US Africa Command Social Science Research Center and is a research fellow with the US Air Force Culture and Language Center. He is a lieutenant colonel in the US Army Reserve, where he is an African foreign area officer and civil affairs officer. He is currently assigned to the 354th Civil Affairs Brigade. In addition to multiple tours in Iraq, he served as a tank platoon leader during Operation Desert Storm, a tank company commander in the 82nd Airborne Division, a deminer in Jordan, chief of host nation liaison in Saudi Arabia, a cease-fire monitor in Sudan, and commander of a civil affairs battalion. He has a PhD in cultural anthropology from the Catholic University of America and a master's in national security studies from the US Army War College. He has published articles with the Foreign Policy Research Institute, PRISM, *Military Review*, and *Practicing Anthropology*.

Index

AAA. *See* American Anthropological Association
Abu Dhabi
   archaeological sites in, 25
   Eagle Resolve exercises in, 18
Abu Ghraib, 18, 129
academic interactions, military interactions and, 115–16
adversary organizational structure, 79
Afghanistan, 49
   cultural information on, x, 5, 8n2, 16–17, 26
   heritage preservation in, 21
Africa
   culture variance in, 114
   fighting terrorism in, 110–14
   humanitarian relief in, 110
   Islam in, 111
   peacekeeping training centers in, 104
   US military development activities in, 110
Africa Command, US (AFRICOM), 102
   noncombat orientation of, 104
   SSRC in JMC, 103–4, 115
   stability operations, 110, 116
AFRICOM. *See* Africa Command, US
Agency for International Development, US, 84
Aginsky, B. W., 2
AIA. *See* Archaeological Institute of America
Air Force, US (USAF), 85
   Culture and Language Center, 117
Algeria culture, 49–50
Allah, Noor, 51–52
Allen, Andi, 51
American Anthropological Association (AAA), ix, 47
   CEAUSSIC of, x, 5, 6, 96, 122
   Code of Ethics, 96–97
   Committee on International Cooperation in Anthropology, 2
   on HTS program, 51
   on military anthropologists as war criminals, 120
   in World War II, 1
American Anthropologist (Aginsky), 2
analysts
   in military intelligence, 87
   program for, 89
Anderson, Ben, 69
animism in Sudan, 105
anthropologist, 3, 59–60. *See also* military anthropologist
   decision making process, 96–97
   in military culture, 17–20
   public, 99
   security, 124
   as technicians, xi
anthropology. *See also* military anthropology
   engagement and, 93–95, 122
   master narratives in, 121–23, 131
   medical, 6
   militarization of, x
   organizational, 93
   as profession, 24–25
   SOF and, 77
   US Naval Academy teaching of, 37

during World War II, 2
"Anthropology and the Military: Charting the Future of Research and Practice," 6
Arabic language, 69
archaeological ethics, 9–28
    on archaeological sites, 12–13, 16, 23, 25–26, 28n3
    human remains research, 14–15
Archaeological Institute of America (AIA), DOD partnership with, 23
archaeological sites
    in Abu Dhabi, 25
    of Babylon, 16, 26, 28n3
    on Fort Drum, 12–13
    in Iraq, 16, 23
    in New England, 13
Army Civil Affairs and Psychological Operations Command, US, 23
Army Peacekeeping Institute, US, 127
Army War Colleges, US, 127
artifact curation facility at Fort Drum, 11
As It Happens (Off), 21
Association of National Committees of the Blue Shield, 26
Athens, Arthur J., 34

Babylon military damage, 16, 26, 28n3
Baggara groups, Muslim
    pastoralism and Islam elements of, 107
    violence of, 108–9
Barnouw, Victor, 48
Bateson, Gregory, 67
Benedict, Ruth, 48
Berber movement, 50
Boas, Franz, 2
Boone, Jim, 69
Brown, Keith, 132

CAOCL. *See* Center for Advanced Operational Culture Learning
cease-fire, 103
    in Nuba Mountains, 101, 107–8
CEAUSSIC. *See* Commission on the Engagement of Anthropology with US Security and Intelligence Communities

Center for Advanced Operational Culture Learning (CAOCL), Marine Corps, 47, 55
Central Command Historical Cultural Action Group (CHCAG), 25
citizen role of military anthropologists, 1, 4
Civil Affairs and Foreign Area Officer Programs, 103
Civil Affairs and Psychological Operations, 77
civil intelligence personnel, 87
civil-military activities of US military, 103
Coast Guard Academy, US, 119
COCOMS. *See* combatant commands
Code of Ethics of AAA, 96–97
Cold War, 3
collegial bucket brigade, 97, 98
collegial interaction, ethics and, 21–23
Colorado State University Center for the Environmental Management of Military Lands, 11
combatant commands (COCOMS), 78, 82n3
Command and Staff College (CSC) at MCU, 53
Commission on the Engagement of Anthropology with US Security and Intelligence Communities (CEAUSSIC), of AAA, x, 5, 6, 96, 122
Committee on International Cooperation in Anthropology, of AAA, 2
computational social science, 79
conflict analysis in Nuba Mountains, 106
contingency operations stewardship by CHCAG, 25
Convention for the Protection of Cultural Properties in the Event of Armed Conflict, 28n5
Cooper, James Fenimore, 67
counterterrorism, 125
CSC. *See* Command and Staff College
cultural information
    in Afghanistan, x, 5, 8n2, 16–17, 26
    in Iraq, x, 5, 8n2, 16–17, 56–57
    military training on, 27
cultural roots of technical transfer failure, 72

culture. *See also* region, culture, and language familiarization program
   Algeria, 49–50
   branch of MCIA, 88
   DOD and, 85
   in GOS, 105
   IC and, 85–86
   Marine Corps, 61–62, 85
   preconflict models of, 103
   -related training, 92
   Sandia safety, 75
   state-centric approach to, 89
   structural-functionalist approach to, 89, 90
   study and integration of, 103
   symbols and rituals in, 33
   of US, 76
   of US Naval Academy, 31–33, 38
   variance in Africa, 114
Culture and Small Wars course at MCU, 46

decision making
   anthropologist process of, 96–97
   ethical by military anthropologist, 25
Defense Threat Reduction Agency, of DOD, 79–80
Democratic Republic of the Congo, sexual- and gender-based violence in, 104
Department of Defense (DOD), 10, 51, 65–66
   AIA partnership with, 23
   culture and, 85
   Defense Threat Reduction Agency, 79–80
   Latin America service work, 122
   Native American consultation policy of, 15
   research funding, 13
Department of Energy nuclear weapons development, 66
Department of Homeland Security, 66, 76, 84
disaster preparedness, 125
disciplinary matrix
   exemplars in, 122
   metaphysical models in, 122
   symbolic generalizations, 122
   values, 122

discussion and questions, shaping at MCIA, 91–92
DOD. *See* Department of Defense
domestic terrorism preparedness. *See* homeland defense
Douglas, Mary, 94, 121, 130

Eagle Reserve exercises in Abu Dhabi, 18
education, 6
   on Islam, 69
   Marine Corps, 100n2
   strategy at MCIA, 91–92
Egypt, on-site training by CHCAG in, 25
"The Empire Speaks Back: US Military and Intelligence Organizations' Perspectives on Engagement with Anthropology" (Fosher/Selmeski), ix, 127
Empire Speaks Back panel war criminals, ix
engagement, anthropology and, 93–95, 122
Errington, Sherry, 67
ethics
   archaeological, 9–28, 28n3
   collegial interaction and, 21–23
   of military anthropology, xi, 8, 95–97
   military archaeology and, 15–17
   negative attention to, 98
ethnicity
   shifting identity and, 101–17
   as unit of analysis, 106
ethnographic focus of SSRC, 104
exemplars in disciplinary matrix, 122
Expeditionary Warfare School at MCU, 54

Facing Mount Kenya (Kenyatta), 115
federal employee oath, 11–12
Ferozi, Abdul Wasi, 26
First to Fight (Krulak), 34
Foreign Language and Area Studies (FLAS), 68
For Official Use Only (FOUO), 87
Fort Drum
   archaeological sites on, 12–13
   artifact curation facility at, 11
   assemblages and landforms at, 13
   LeRay estate historic district, 12

predeployment training in negotiation at, 127
Tenth Mountain Division, 11, 15
Forte, Maximilian, 129
Forward Operating Base Hammer, 28n4
Fosher, Kerry, ix–x, 53, 56, 123–25, 127, 129, 132n4
  on organizational reshaping, 84
FOUO. *See* For Official Use Only
Freedom of Information Act, 87
Fujimura, Clementine, 30
Fulbright-Hayes Act (1961), 82n1

González, Roberto, 132
Geertz, Clifford, 67, 78
Gibson, MacGuire, 23
global counter insurgency, xi
Global Maritime Partnerships, 43
Global War on Terror, 78, 111
GOS. *See* Sudan, government of
Greenhouse, Carol, 69
group diversity, 7
Guistozzi, Antonio, 51–52
Guttman, Matthew, 132

Hague Convention for the Protection of Cultural Property during Times of Armed Conflict (2008), 17
Harris, Marvin, 115
Hawass, Zahi, 25
Henry, Jules, 3
heritage preservation
  in Afghanistan, 21
  in Iraq, 21
  during military operations, 25
  US military funding of, 26
heritage property in war zones, 21
Hersh, Seymour, 129
Hickey, Gerald, 4
historical analysis, 123
Holmes-Weber, Paula, 59–60, 85
homeland defense, 83
Houtman, Gustaaf, 130
HTS. *See* Human Terrain System
humanitarian demining, 109
humanitarian relief

  in Africa, 110
  in military operations, 18, 52, 84, 102
human osteology, 14
human remains research, archaeological ethics and, 14–15
Human Terrain System (HTS), x, 8n2, 63n1, 128
  AAA on, 51
  on anthropologists military embedded, 5

IC. *See* intelligence community
identity
  language and, 50
  Nuba Mountains and, 106
  shifting, ethnicity and, 101–17
Illinois River valley Native American burial mounds, 13
imperialism, 3
infrastructure, peacekeeping operations and, 105
initiative products, 88
intelligence community (IC), 6, 83. *See also* Marine Corps Intelligence Activity
  culture and, 85–86
  FOUO designation by, 87
  initiative products of, 88
  open source materials for, 87
  state-centric approach to culture in, 89
  structural-functionalist approach to culture in, 89, 90
International Military Cultural Resources Working Group, 25–26
international relations during Cold War, 3
Iraq
  archaeological sites in, 16, 23
  city of Ur, 26
  cultural information on, x, 5, 8n2, 16–17, 56–57
  heritage preservation in, 21
  military withdrawal in, 114
  Shiite uprising in, 103
Islam. *See also* Muslims
  conversion, 111
  education on, 69
  element of Baggara groups, 107
  extremism in Muslim area of Sudan, 111

ideological control in GOS, 112
Israeli Military Psychology Center, 56

Jackson School of International Studies at University of Washington, 59
  Anthropology of the Middle East and Islam course at, 45–46
JMC. *See* Joint Military Commission
Johnston, Rob, 100n1
Joint Forces Staff College, 127
Joint Military Commission (JMC), 101–2
  AFRICOM SSRC and, 103–4, 115
Joint Special Operations University (JSOU), 77–78
Jorgensen, Joseph, 4
JSOU. *See* Joint Special Operations University
just and unjust wars, military archaeologists on, 16
Justice and Equality Movement in Darfur, 116

Keenan, Jeremy, 124–27, 129, 132n4
Keesing, Roger, 67
Kenyatta, Jomo, 115–16
Kila, Joris, 25
Kirsch, Tom, 68
Krulak, Victor H., 34
Kuhn, Thomas, 121–22

Ladenheim, Gina, 51
land management strategies, military operation and, 20
land mine removal in Nuba Mountains, 109–10
  humanitarian efforts for, 109
  victims' assistance and public awareness campaigns, 109
language. *See also* region, culture, and language familiarization program
  Arabic, 69
  identity and, 50
  Swahili in Tanzania, 112
"Language Skills, Regional Expertise and Cultural Awareness Strategy," 43
The Last of the Mohicans (Cooper), 67

Latin America
  DOD service work, 122
  Project Camelot in, 122
Latour, Bruno, 123
Leadership, Ethics, and Law (LEL) department at US Naval Academy, 37
legitimization concept for military archaeologists, 16
LEL. *See* Leadership, Ethics, and Law
LeRay estate historic district at Fort Drum, 12
Lucas, George, 6, 122
Lutz, Catherine, 132

Malinowski, B., 122
Marine Corps, 129
  CAOCL, 47, 55
  culture, 61–62, 85
  culture center, 116–17
  TECOM in, 89
  training and education, 100n2
  values, 46
Marine Corps Intelligence Activity (MCIA), 53, 85, 89
  anthropology, 93
  contextual factors, 86–88
  culture branch of, 88
  current change in, 86
  direct support to operations, 90–91
  education strategy, 91–92
  information by, 87–88
  occupational categories in, 94
  product and design and review, 90
  shaping discussion and questions at, 91–92
  vignettes development by, 80
  visualization tools at, 90
Marine Corps University (MCU), 45
  Culture and Small Wars course at, 46
  OCS on, 47
  Operational Culture for Strategists course at, 46
  professor of operational culture, 60–62
  SAW at, 48–49
Marine Corps War College (MCWAR), 54
maritime technology at Fort Drum archaeological site, 13

master narratives in anthropology, 121–23, 131
Matthes, Melissa, 119–20
Maxwell School of Citizenship and Public Affairs, of Syracuse University, ix, 6
MCIA. *See* Marine Corps Intelligence Activity
McNamara, Laura, 129, 130
MCU. *See* Marine Corps University
MCWAR. *See* Marine Corps War College
Mead, Margaret, 3
medical anthropology, 6
Mesopotamia, military archaeology and, 16, 26
metaphysical models in disciplinary matrix, 122
metonymic reduction, 126–28
military, US. *See also specific branches*
 on adversary organizational structure, 79
 Babylon damage by, 16, 26, 28n3
 civil-military activities, 103
 culture, anthropologist/archaeologist in, 17–20
 development activities in Africa, 110
 heritage preservation funding by, 26
 intelligence, 83–100
 as operational organization, 81
 social science and, 92–93
 Somalia involvement by, 103
 values, 20–21
 withdrawal in Iraq, 114
military anthropologist
 citizen role of, 1, 4
 education and training domain, 6
 ethical decision making of, 25
 on group diversity, 7
 intelligence domain, 6
 operational support domain, 6
 policy development domain, 6
 as profession, 24–25
 public anthropologist and, 99
 studied people harm and, 2
 as war criminals, 120
military anthropology
 benefits and harm from, 2
 challenges, 122
 on effective communication, 80
 ethics of, xi, 8, 95–97
 exploring, 1–8
 nature and importance of, 41–43
military archaeologists, 9–28
 on just and unjust wars, 16
 legitimization concept for, 16
 military operations and, 17
military archaeology
 ethics and, 15–17
 Mesopotamia and, 16, 26
military interactions, academic interactions and, 114–16
military operations
 cultural specialists in, 101–17
 direct support for, 90–91
 heritage preservation during, 25
 humanitarian relief in, 18, 52, 84, 102
 land management strategies and, 20
 land mine removal, 109–10
 military archaeologists and, 17
 nation building in, 18
 for natural disaster, 25, 55
 negative impact on civilians during, 102
military training
 on cultural information, 27
 land management, 9
Muslims. *See also* Islam
 area in Sudan, Islamic extremism in, 111
 Baggara groups, 106–9
 in Sudan, 105–6

National Defense Education Act (1958), FLAS of, 82n1
National Science Foundation, 10, 124
national security community, xi, 1, 65–66, 81
 after 9/11, 66, 76
 organizations and, 83
 Turnley work with, 75
nation building in military operations, 18
Native American
 burial mounds in Illinois River valley, 13
 consultation policy, of DOD, 15
 consultation program, 10, 13–15

human remains excavation and study, 14–15
Native American Graves Protection and Repatriation Act (1990), 11
natural disasters
　cultural property planning information on, 25
　for military operations, 25, 55
Naval Academy, US
　anthropology taught at, 37
　culture of, 31–33, 38
　LEL department at, 37
　ritual structure of, 35
　subculture of, 39–40
Navy, US
　Maritime Civil Affairs Group, 117
　ritual in, 33–34
New England
　archaeological sites in, 13
　Center for Emergency Preparedness, 84
NGOs. See nongovernmental organizations
9/11, 83–84
　national security community after, 66, 76
　social networks after, 78
noncombat orientation of AFRICOM, 104
nongovernmental organizations (NGOs), 105
Nuba Mountains in Sudan
　acts of violence in, 108
　cease-fire in, 107–8
　conflict analysis in, 106
　land mine removal, 109–10
　Muslims in, 105–6
　peacekeeping operations in, 105–9
　Shatt area of, 107
　SPLA cease-fire agreement for, 101
　UN programs and, 105
nuclear weapons, 66
Nyerere, Julius, 112, 114

occupational categories in MCIA, 94
OCS. See Officer Candidates School
Off, Carol, 21
Officer Candidates School (OCS), 47, 58
open source materials for IC, 87

Operational Culture for Strategies course at MCU, 46
organizational anthropology, 93
organization reshaping, 84

pastoralism of Baggara groups, 107
Patal, Raphael, 129
PDF. See Popular Defense Forces
peacekeeping operations
　cease-fire and, 101, 103, 107–8
　future increase in, 116
　in Nuba Mountains of Central Sudan, 105–9
　poor infrastructure and, 105
　training centers in Africa, 104
policy development, 6
Popular Defense Forces (PDF), 108
Price, David, 132
product design and review at MCIA, 90, 98
Project Camelot, 122
public anthropologist, 99
public awareness campaigns for land mind removal, 109

Rappaport, Roy, 68
RCLF. See region, culture, and language familiarization
Redfield, Robert, 3
region, culture, and language familiarization (RCLF) program
　curriculum, 56
　at Marine Corps University, 50
religion. See also Islam; Muslims
　in GOS, 112–13
　in Tanzania, 111–12
research. See also Social Science Research Center
　funding by DOD, 13
　human remains, 14–15
　manipulation in social science, 115
Reserve Officer Training Corps, 34
retrospective attribution, 123–26, 131
ritual
　classification of stages of, 35–36
　in culture, 33
　pollution, 129–31

structure of US Naval Academy, 35
  in US Navy, 33–34
Rose, Brian, 23
Rubinstein, Robert, ix, 33, 83, 103

Saddam Hussein, 16, 26
Samoff, Joel, 106
Sandia, 72–73
  safety culture in, 75
SAW. *See* School of Advanced Warfighting
scholarly community, SSRC on relations cultivation with, 104
School of Advanced Warfighting (SAW)
  at Marine Corps University, 48–49
  as military science master program, 49
School of Oriental and African Studies, 124, 131
security anthropologist, 124
Selmeski, Brian, ix–x, 84, 127
Shari law in GOS, 106
Shiite uprising in Iraq, 103
shura, 26, 28n7
Siegel, Jim, 69
Small, Cathy, 42
social networks after 9/11, 78
social science, 2
  computational, 79
  military, US and, 92–93
  research manipulation, 115
Social Science Research Center (SSRC), 102
  AFRICOM and, 103–4, 115
  ethnographic focus of, 104
  research examples, 104
  on scholarly community relations cultivation, 104
Society for Applied Anthropology, 72
SOF. *See* special operations forces
Somalia, US military involvement in, 103
special operations forces (SOF), 77, 82n3
SPLA. *See* Sudan People's Liberation Army
SSRC. *See* Social Science Research Center
stability operations of AFRICOM, 110, 116
Stanford, Dennis, 13, 28n2
state-centric approach to culture, 89
Stout, Katie, 51

"Strategic Plan for Language Skills, Regional Expertise and Cultural Capabilities 2011-2016" (US Department of Defense), 51
structural-functionalist approach to culture, 89, 90
subculture of US Naval Academy, 39–40
Sudan, government of (GOS). *See also* Nuba Mountains in Sudan
  animism in, 105
  culture, 105
  Islam ideological control in, 112
  Muslims in, 105–6
  religion in, 112–13
  Shari law in, 106
  SPLA fighting with, 106
Sudan People's Liberation Army (SPLA), 105
  cease-fire agreement for Nuba Mountains, 101
  GOS fighting with, 106
Supreme Council of Egyptian Antiquities, 25
symbolic generalizations in disciplinary matrix, 122
symbols, 33
Syracuse University symposium, x

Tanzania
  religion in, 111–12
  Swahili language in, 112
Tax, Sol, 3
teaching and mentoring at MCIA, 89
technicians, anthropologists as, xi
technology transfer, 71
  cultural roots of failure of, 72
TECOM. *See* Training and Education Command
Tenth Mountain Division, of Fort Drum, 11, 15
terrorism
  counter, 125
  fighting, in Africa, 110–14
training, 6
  CHCAG in Egypt, 25
  culture-related, 92
  Fort Drum predeployment on negotiations, 127

Marine Corps, 100n2
military, 9, 27
peacekeeping centers in Africa, 104
Training and Education Command (TECOM), 89
"Training Female Engagement Teams: Framework, Content Development, and Lessons Learned" (Allen, Ladenheim, Stout), 51
"Tribes" and Warlords in Southern Afghanistan 1980-2005 (Guistozzi/Allah), 51–52
Turnley, Jessica Glicken
  national security community work, 75
  Sandia employment by, 72–73
  WESSTcorp of, 71–72, 75, 81

UN. *See* United Nations
Under Construction: Making Homeland Security at the Local Level (Fosher), 123–25, 132n4
United Nations (UN), 127
  Nuba Mountains and, 105
United States (US). *See also* military, US
  Agency for International Development, 84
  culture of, 76
Ur, Iraq, 26
US. *See* United States
USAF. *See* Air Force, US
US Special Operations Command (USSOCOM), 77–78, 82n3

core activities of, 82n4
as formal organization, 79

values
  in disciplinary matrix, 122
  Marine Corps, 46
  US military, 20–21
Vice Admiral James B. Stockdale Center for Ethical Leadership, 34
victims' assistance campaigns, land mine removal and, 109
violence
  of Baggara groups, 108–9
  in Democratic Republic of Congo, 104
  in Nuba Mountains in Sudan, 108
The Virginian (Wister), 67
visualization tools at MCIA, 90

WAC. *See* World Archaeology Congress
war criminals, ix, 120
WESSTcorp, 71–72, 75, 81
White, Leslie, 68
Wister, Owen, 67
Wolf, Eric, 4
Wolfe, Robert, 3–4
World Archaeology Congress (WAC), military archaeologists at, 21–23
World War II
  AAA meeting during, 1
  anthropology during, 2

Also available from Kumarian Press

Sustainable Capitalism: A Matter of Common Sense
John Ikerd

"For years, John Ikerd's writings and speeches have provided precious insights into the economics of this nation's food system, exploding the myth that factory farms are economically imperative. In this brilliant book, he makes a powerful case for a new capitalistic economy: one that is environmentally sound, socially just, and economically sustainable." —*Robert F. Kennedy, Jr.*

The Myth of the Free Market: The Role of the State in a Capitalist Economy
Mark A. Martinez

"In this thoughtful and erudite book, Mark Martinez forces us to re-examine the myth of the 'natural' free market order. Using very intelligently a wide range of fascinating historical and contemporary examples, he takes us through many important economic, political, and philosophical reflections about the true nature of the market system and its important but limited role in the construction of a civilized society." —*Ha-Joon Chang, University of Cambridge, author of* Kicking Away the Ladder *and* Bad Samaritans

"Explains the role of political processes in creating and supporting capitalist markets." —*Publishers Weekly*

The Great Turning: From Empire to Earth Community
David C. Korten

"A work of amazing scope and depth that shows we can create cultures where our enormous human capacities for joy, caring, and cooperation are realized." —*Riane Eisler, author of* The Chalice and the Blade

Kumarian Press
An Imprint of Stylus Publishing
22883 Quicksilver Drive
Sterling, VA 20166-2102

Subscribe to our e-mail alerts: www.kpbooks.com

Kumarian Press, located in Sterling, Virginia, is a forward-looking, scholarly press that promotes active international engagement and an awareness of global connectedness.